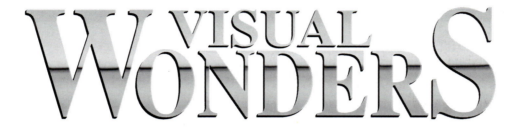

VISUAL WONDERS

Ships, Trains, and Planes

VISUAL WONDERS

Ships, Trains, and Planes

Written by
Richard Humble, Julian Holland, and Ian Graham

WHITECAP BOOKS
VANCOUVER/TORONTO/NEW YORK

ACKNOWLEDGMENTS

Illustrated by
Julian Baker, John Batchelor, Chris Brown, Peter Bull, Bob Corley,
Anthony Cowland, John Dunne, Robert Farnworth, Dave Fisher, Mick Gillah,
David Graham, Terry Hadler, Nick Hawker, Paul Higgens, Christian Hook,
Graham Humphreys, Ray Hutchins, Steve Lach, Stuart Lafford, Ian Lowe, Brian
McIntyre, Ernest Nisbet, Steve Noon, Julia Osorno, Darren Pattenden, Roger
Payne, Steve Seymour, Tony Smith, Clive Spong, Roger Stewart,
Alan Weston, Brian Warson, Gerald Whitcomb, Sean Wilkinson.

Picture credits
58 (top left) Venice-Simplon Orient Express Ltd, 77 (top left), 77 (bottom right)
London Regional Transport Contract 96-2409 Registered user,
86 (bottom left), 99 (top left) Imperial War Museum,
108 (center left) Lockheed Advanced Development Company.

Editor Jenny Fry
Cover design Alix Wood

The Publishers would also like to thank the following for their assistance
Air France, France; Boeing International, USA; Books International, England;
British Airways, England; Bundesarchiv, Germany; Canadair, Canada; Cutty Sark
Museum, England; French Naval Public Relations Office, England;
French Embassy – Defense and Naval Attaché, London; Imperial War
Museum, England; Lockheed Advanced Development Company, USA;
London Transport Museum, England; Marine Nationale, France; RAF
Museum, England; Rolls Royce, England; Venice-Simplon Orient Express Ltd,
England; The Puffing Billy Railway Information Service, USA; Queen Mary
Archives, England.

This edition first published in the United States and Canada by Whitecap Books.

Whitecap Books Ltd
Vancouver Office,
351 Lynn Avenue, North Vancouver, BC
Canada V7J 2C4

Whitecap Books
Toronto Office,
47 Coldwater Road, North York, ON
Canada M3B 1Y8

Graphic Arts Center Publishing
P.O. Box 10306, Portland, OR
USA 97296-0306

Planned and produced by
Andromeda Oxford Limited
11–13 The Vineyard
Abingdon
Oxon
OX14 3PX

Copyright © 2000 Andromeda Oxford Limited

ISBN 1-55110-988-3

Printed in Italy by Milanostampa.

Contents

Number "9"

Number "4"

"About to set sail"

What is a ship?

Ships have carried people and their goods across the seas and oceans of the world since the dawn of history. Even in the modern age of air and space travel, ships remain as vital to world trade and transport as ever. As well as cargo and passenger-carrying ships, fighting warships have always been needed to control the world's sea-trading routes. Since the days of Ancient Egypt, Greece and Rome, the sea power provided by ships has built and pulled down empires around the world. This book describes every important stage in the development of the ship from earliest times. Because many of these ships were later modified, we often picture more than one version to show the variety of designs that were available.

FLAGS

For hundreds of years ships have flown flags to identify themselves and to send messages to other ships. Every flag has its own meaning.

WHO'S WHO

There were about 850 officers and crew aboard an eighteenth-century battleship.

① ② ③ ④ ⑤ ⑥

1. Captain   2. Lieutenant   3. Midshipman
4. Seaman   5. Gunner   6. Powderboy

OAR AND SAIL

From about 2500 B.C. to the 1500s A.D., both oars and sails were used for driving ships. The ship below is a Greek trireme of about 500 B.C.

Yard supporting sail

Stern

Tiller connecting steering oars

Rowers

Deck

Bow

Ram

Oars

AGE OF THE FIGHTING SAIL

A three-decked wooden sailing battleship, armed with up to 100 guns or more, was the most powerful of all warships from about 1630 to 1850. The picture on the right identifies the main masts and some of the sails used to rig this type of ship.

Mainmast

Foremast

Jib

Bowsprit

Spritsail

Keel

LUXURY AFLOAT

Modern passenger liners have luxury cabins, cinemas, restaurants, swimming pools, and playrooms for children. Safety is also important. For most of their history, ships were highly dangerous to sail in. "Lifeboats for all on board" has only been compulsory since the liner *Titanic* was sunk by an iceberg in 1912, causing 1,498 crew and passengers to drown.

Streamlined funnel

Lifeboats

Bridge

Passenger saloon

Rudder

Propeller

Fin to stop ship rolling

THE SHIP'S CREW

A modern ship's "complement" (officers and crew) includes people with many different skills: navigators, computer operators, engine-room mechanics and, of course, a good cook!

1. Captain 2. Navigator 3. Radio operator
4. Nurse 5. Mechanic 6. Cook

Mizzenmast

Stern windows

Gun decks

Stores in lower holds

Hull

HOW A SHIP WORKS

A ship's hull pushes away, or displaces, a weight of water equal to its own weight. Trying to return to its original position, the displaced water pushes the ship up. The picture on the right shows how this allows a ship to float.

Air pressure

Water pressure

PROPULSION

The angled blades of the ship's propeller make the propeller screw its way forward, pushing the ship in front of it.

Some modern high-speed ferries use jet propulsion, sucking in seawater and driving it out in a high-speed water jet.

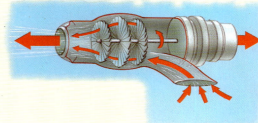

STEERING

The hinged rudder at the ship's stern is attached to the wheel or tiller. If the helmsman pushes the tiller to the left (port), the rudder and bow move to the right (starboard). If he wants the ship to go to the right, he moves the tiller to the left.

Amidships

A-port (left)

A-starboard (right)

TACKING AGAINST THE WIND

During the age of sail, arrangements of sails were developed that made it possible to sail "close to the wind." By turning or tacking from side to side, a ship could progress without relying on winds from behind.

Development and uses of ships

Down the centuries, ships have changed human destiny again and again. They have carried people in search of new lands in which to live and new markets from which to profit through trade. Side by side with the development of merchant ships, warships have defended trade and conquered enemy fleets. Even in the space age, nearly 5,000 years since the first recorded ships put to sea, ships are still carrying the world's heaviest cargoes and offering passengers luxurious conditions for long-distance travel.

DEVELOPMENT

Designers have constantly looked for ways of improving ships. From single sails to diesel engines, ships have become safer, more comfortable and faster.

HULL DESIGN

For nearly 5,000 years, hulls were built of wood. At first people hollowed out trees. Later, they fixed planks together, overlapping them (clinker) and then laying them side by side (carvel). In the Industrial Revolution, iron and steel were utilized. Today, ships are constructed from materials such as GRP (glass-reinforced plastic).

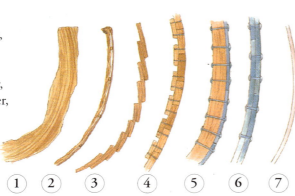

1. Wooden dug-out
2. Pegged planks
3. Clinker style
4. Carvel style
5. Ironclad
6. Riveted steel plates
7. GRP

NAVIGATIONAL INSTRUMENTS

Early navigational aids measured the ship's course and its position north or south of the equator by measuring the angle between the Sun or stars and the ship. Examples are the astrolabe and the sextant. Today, people use electronics, computers and satellite technology.

1. Astrolabe
2. Sextant
3. Compass
4. Radar
5. Satellite navigation

SAILS DEVELOP

The Egyptians drove their ships, such as the "round" ship, with a single square sail. This was the only sort of sail used until the Middle Ages, when traders adopted the designs of sails on Chinese junks and Arab dhows. By the seventeenth century, ships had many masts and sails.

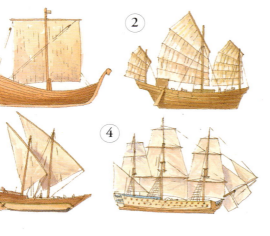

1. "Round" ship
2. Chinese junk
3. Arab dhow
4. Ship of the line

PROPULSION

In the nineteenth century, steam power freed ships from the uncertainties of wind, tides and currents. First came side paddlewheels. In the middle of the century, they were superseded by the more efficient stern screw propeller. The latest high-speed drive is the water jet.

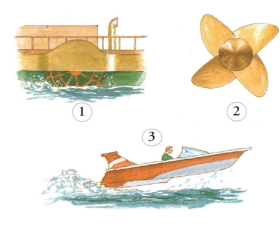

1. Side paddlewheel
2. Screw propeller
3. Water jet

SHIPS DOWN THE AGES

The most dramatic changes in the design of both trading ships and warships have taken place in the last 200 years. From the third millennium B.C. until the beginning of the nineteenth century A.D., ships were driven only by oar or sail.

3000 B.C.: First known ship: Egyptian reed boat

1180 B.C.: First known warship: Egyptian war galley

A.D. 150: Roman merchant ship: used for trading throughout the empire

850: Viking longship: development of clinker-style hull

1490: Spanish caravel: development of carvel-style hull, with three masts

USES

Ships are used in a variety of human activities: trade, warfare, emigration, exploration, scientific research, leisure and tourism, life-saving, fishing – even agriculture. The pictures below illustrate some of the different activities in which ships are involved.

PASSENGER SHIPS

Different types of ship exist to transport people across the seaways. Ferries, hovercraft and hydrofoils enable passengers to cross seas quickly and efficiently taking their own transport with them. Passenger liners were developed at the end of the last century as one of the most luxurious forms of travel. They are no longer able to compete with jet airliners for speed or price, although ocean liners, shown above, are used for luxury holidays.

TRADE AND COMMERCE

Ships play a vital part in a nation's ability to trade by importing or exporting a variety of cargoes. Cargo ships include tankers that carry crude oil and container ships that carry solid goods. Ships are also used for obtaining resources from the sea. The picture to the right shows a trawler. It drags its nets through the sea to trap fish.

MILITARY SHIPS

Military ships can be used as a base for troops and weapons. For example, aircraft carriers provide a fully equipped air base. Military ships are also used for attacking enemy targets. For example, ships such as the French destroyer *Tourville*, shown above, carry guided missiles.

RESCUE SHIPS

Each maritime nation has its own rescue service, and lifeboats play an essential part of this. The picture to the left shows a lifeboat setting out to rescue passengers and crew from a shipping disaster. The lifeboat is launched down a slipway from the lifeboat station into the sea. It uses radar to find the ship in distress.

1570–1620: Development of broadside-firing galleon: emerged as leading warship

1802: Scottish *Charlotte Dundas*: first working steamship

1859: Development of ironclads: the *Monitor* (launched 1862) introduced rotating armored turrets

1897: British *Turbinia*: first ship with turbine engines

1906: *Dreadnought* battleship: carried ten heavy guns, transforming battleship design

1923: First aircraft carriers enter service: British *Hermes* is one of these

1920s and 1930s: Development of luxury liners: *Queen Mary* (launched 1934) was the largest of these

1960s: Development of guided-missile warships

1990 *Hoverspeed Great Britain*: world's largest multi-hull jet ferry

Egyptian warship

"I caused the Nile mouth to be prepared like a strong wall with warships and galleys . . . a net was prepared for the enemy, to ensnare them."
Pharaoh Ramses III,
Medinet Habu victory monument

Ancient Egypt was the world's first sea power, building cargo ships for trade and fighting ships for war. Egypt's first sailing ships were built of papyrus reeds, but by 2500 B.C. Egypt was building elegant river boats and ships of cedar wood imported from Lebanon. The world's oldest surviving ship (about 2500 B.C.) is the cedar-built funeral barge of Pharaoh Cheops, builder of the Great Pyramid. Defeating the invading "Sea Peoples" with a fleet of war galleys, shown below, Pharaoh Ramses III won the first known sea battle in about 1180 B.C. The pictures of the battle on the walls of Ramses III's temple at Medinet Habu show that it was won not only by the ramming attacks of the Egyptians but also by hand-to-hand fighting to board and capture enemy ships. This would remain an important part of naval warfare for the next 3,000 years, until long-range guns and explosive shells came into use in the nineteenth century.

REED SHIPS

Papyrus reeds, growing beside the Nile River, provided pith for Ancient Egyptian paper-making. When lashed together in tight bundles, papyrus also provided the world's first sea-going sailing ships. These were built over 5,000 years ago.

WEAPONS

On both land and sea, the main Egyptian weapons were bows and arrows for long-range fire, javelins, war clubs, swords and maces, and light battle-axes made of bronze.

BUILDING THE HULL

Egyptian builders constructed hulls by pegging together short lengths of plank. Crossbeams ran across the hulls. Decking planks were laid on the crossbeams and the sailors and teams of rowers lived and worked above these.

Steering oar

Archers firing at enemy ship

Mast backstay

12

CAULKING THE SEAMS

The joints, or seams, between the outer planks were caulked, or made watertight, by packing oiled papyrus reeds into them.

Masthead lookout post

Single sail
The ship could not be steered into a headwind.

Rowing benches
These were protected by raised side-planking

Single oar
A large oar steered the ship.

An Egyptian war galley of this type, rowing 12 oars a side, was probably about 70ft. (21m) long from the tip of the ram to the stern. Apart from its crew of 24 rowers it could have carried about 20 archers and soldiers.

Bronze-covered ram
For attacking enemy ships

Sail "brailed" up to yard

Mast forestay (broken)

Single fixed mast

THE FIRST KNOWN NAVAL BATTLE

After the funeral barge of Pharaoh Cheops was carefully taken to pieces and buried with him for use in the afterlife, over 1,300 years passed before the Egyptians recorded their first victory in a battle at sea. The memorial temple of Ramses III at Medinet Habu shows detailed pictures of the battle, with the war galleys of Egypt defeating the fleet of the "Sea Peoples." The battle was fought off the mouth of the Nile River. The Egyptians won it by ramming and sinking some of the enemy ships and capturing others by boarding them with soldiers.

THE DEADLY RAM

The ram was a forward-jutting extension of the ship's keel, usually armored with a heavy bronze cap in the shape of an animal's head.

Greek trireme

"They could not clear their oars in the rough sea, which made the ships more difficult for the steersmen to handle. The Athenians attacked, and after sinking one of the admiral's ships, went on to destroy every ship that they came across."
Thucydides, *History of the Peloponnesian War*

The Ancient Greeks perfected the war galley with their trireme, which means "three oars." During Egypt's decline, and eventual conquest by Persia in 525 B.C., the Phoenicians rose as a new sea power. They introduced the bireme, which had two banks of oars on each side instead of the one bank used by the Egyptians. By 500 B.C. the Greeks had added a third bank of oars and created a faster, deadly naval weapon.

Triremes put to sea under sail, and often cruised hundreds of miles before sighting the enemy. The mast and sail would then be lowered, and rowers took over so that the trireme could ram enemy ships and sink them. The trireme fleets of Athens and Sparta smashed Persia's invasion of Greece in 480 B.C. Over 200 Persian ships were lost in exchange for less than 40 Greek ones. Later, in the Peloponnesian War between Athens and Sparta (431–404 B.C.), there were many battles between trireme fleets. Spartan triremes claimed the final sea victory.

WARRIORS AT SEA

A trireme carried heavily armored foot soldiers called hoplites. Armed with spears and swords, they fought on land as well as on warships at sea.

ROWING ON THREE LEVELS

Scholars argued for hundreds of years over how triremes were actually rowed. It was not until a replica trireme was built in the 1980s, with the help of computer design, that the mystery was solved. The trireme was rowed by 170 men, 85 on each side. The oars of the 31 *thranites* on the top bank were carried clear of the lower two banks by an outrigger extension from the ship's side. Below them were 27 *zygites* of the middle bank and 27 *thalamites* of the bottom bank.

"All-seeing eye"

"ALL-SEEING EYE"

Above the bronze-capped ram, the forepost swept up in an elegant curve. The bow was painted with an "all-seeing eye," one of the oldest good-luck charms in the history of seafaring. The eye was supposed to guide the ship on its way and bring it safely back to harbor. It is shown in paintings of ancient Egyptian ships of about 2400 B.C., and is still carried by the fishing boats of many nations today.

Mast and sail
Mast raised and sail set for cruising; lowered in battle

Outrigger
This special device stretched out from the ship's side. It enabled a ship to carry more than one bank of oars.

Ram
Sharp ram at the end of the trireme's bow, used to punch holes in enemy ships

Twin stern oars
For steering ship

The trireme's maximum size was 121ft. (37m) long and 20ft. (6m) across.

CAPTAIN AND OFFICERS

The trireme's captain, called a *trierarch*, commanded the ship from a seat in the stern. He was surrounded by soldiers and officers, and in front stood the steersman. The captain had to make sure the rowers had enough strength for the burst of speed needed for a ramming attack.

SKILLED ROWERS

Rowing a trireme was a highly skilled task. The tips of the oar blades were only 12in. (30cm) apart, and the work was all the harder because only the top bank of rowers could see the water.

Hoplite soldier

Steersman

Tiller

Trierarch

Roman merchant ship

"The crew was like an army. They told me she could carry enough grain to satisfy every mouth in Athens for a whole year. And the whole fortune of the ship is in the hands of a little old man who moves the great rudders with a tiller no thicker than a stick."
Lucian

The Greek writer Lucian wrote the above words in about A.D. 150. He was describing a Roman merchant ship at the port of Athens, then part of the Roman Empire. These ships were tough and seaworthy. They carried a wide range of cargo, and the biggest were fitted with passenger cabins in the stern. The cabins could hold more than 250 people, and these were often prisoners or slaves, shackled and crammed together with no regard for their comfort. Since the ships rarely sailed during the stormy winter months, the crew usually slept on deck.

STERNPOST

At the stern of Roman merchant ships, the tall, curving sternpost was topped by a graceful swan's or goose's head. Like the carved figureheads on ships of later centuries, it was painted and gilded.

ROMAN EMPIRE

Rome's empire, shown in orange on the map on the left, depended on trade by sea. Merchant fleets cruised the Mediterranean Sea, sailed along the Atlantic coast of Spain and France, and sailed across the English Channel.

SPREADING THE PLAGUE

Rats often swarmed in the cargo holds of Roman ships carrying grain. The rats carried the plague and helped to spread the disease. It swept across the Roman Empire from the Middle East in A.D. 166.

Mainmast

Spritsail

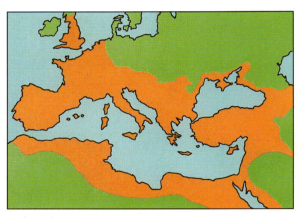

16

FEEDING THE EMPIRE

Food was brought to Rome and other cities by ship. Egypt was one of the Roman Empire's most important corn-growing provinces. Grain was carried in sacks, and wine and olive oil in tall earthenware jars called amphorae.

A merchant ship of the 2nd Century A.D. was about 180ft. (55m) long, 46ft. (14m) wide and 43ft. (13m) from deck to keel.

Mainsail
The ship was driven by a large square sail.

Artemon mast
Carried the small bow spritsail, which was used to help steering

Swan's head
Ships often had a carved swan's head, representing the Egyptian goddess Isis, protector of sailors

Steering oars
There were two, each with its own tiller

Cargo hold
Cargo included wine, oil, grain and cloth.

RICH TRADERS

Successful merchants and bankers were the richest men in the Roman empire. Many of them made fortunes from shipping the vital cargoes on which the empire depended. They lived in great luxury and held enormous power, for even emperors needed to borrow their money. Some rich merchants succeeded in becoming the emperor of Rome by using their wealth to buy the support of imperial soldiers.

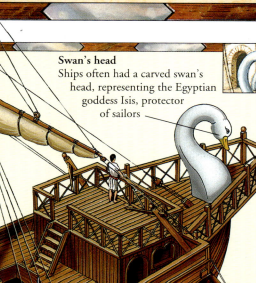

Tiller

Poopdeck

Poopdeck shelter

ANIMAL TRANSPORT

Wild animals such as panthers and lions were shipped to major cities from Africa and the Middle East. They were taken to Roman amphitheaters, to be used in fighting contests. The caged animals were handled at the docks by slave workers.

Viking longship

"See where the great longship proudly lies at anchor. Above the prow, the dragon rears its glowing head. The bows were bound with gold after the hull was launched."
Saga of Harold Hadrada

FIGUREHEAD
Some longships had an elaborately carved animal on the forepost – the pointed structure built up from the ship's bow. This figurehead, originally covered in gold leaf, is from a beautifully decorated funeral ship found in Norway.

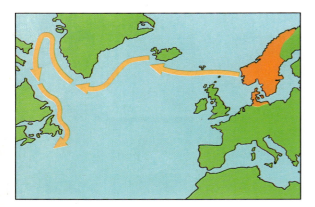

ATLANTIC EXPLORATION
Longships carried Viking explorers across the North Atlantic Ocean to the Faroes, Iceland, Greenland and to North America, which the Vikings called "Vinland." The orange shading on the map above shows the Viking empire.

WEATHER VANE
Made of gilded bronze, this intricate weather vane is a superb example of Viking art. It once flew at the head of a longship's mast. Weather vanes were used to show the steersman the direction of the wind.

After the fall of the Roman Empire, the Viking longship emerged as the most important vessel of the open seas. First recorded in the late 700s, the longship was built in Denmark, Norway and Sweden. It carried Viking warriors to plunder every country in western Europe and Russia, as well as North America.

Like the ancient Egyptians, the Vikings sometimes buried ships at warriors' funerals, and several have been found and studied. A famous longship found at Gokstad, in Norway, is 75ft. (23m) long. Like all Viking ships, it was clinker-built, which means that its hull was made from overlapping planks. It sailed well and, by lowering its single mast and sail, could also be rowed. It was narrow and sat shallow in the water, which meant that it could be rowed up rivers with ease. The Gokstad longship was rowed by 16 rowers each side. The Vikings used their sea chests as rowing benches. Many longships were much bigger than the Gokstad; the *Ormen Lange*, or "Long Serpent," owned by King Olaf Tryggvason of Norway (995–1000), had 34 oars on each side.

WARRIOR
A Viking warrior's main weapons were a battle-ax and a long sword. Wealthier warriors wore a helmet and a shirt of linked iron rings.

Steersman

Steering oar

THE HULL

The hull of a longship like the Gokstad ship, shown above, had 16 overlapping planks on each side to make it strong enough to withstand the heavy seas. During building, the ship was held firmly in place on land as the curved planks were added.

Square sail
Tough woolen cloth strengthened with strips of material, such as leather

Chest
Used as a rowing bench

Steering oar
On the starboard, or right-hand, side of the ship

Storage space
Extra food, water, tools and timber were stored under the deck.

This longship is 69ft. (21m) long and 16ft. (5m) across at its widest point. It has oar holes for 15 pairs of rowers.

Lowered sail

Forepost

FINAL VOYAGE

A Viking warrior dreaded the thought of dying in his bed, and dreamed of falling in battle. Some Vikings were buried on land in their ships, while others were burned aboard ship surrounded by their weapons.

Hansa trading cog

"The French put their ships in readiness, like the skilled seamen and good fighters they were, and set the cog Christopher, which they had taken from the English that same year, in the van with a big company of Genoese crossbowmen on board to defend it and harass the English."
Jean Froissart, *Chronicles*, 1340

A new kind of ship began to appear in Europe from about 1250. Called a cog, it still had many features used by earlier shipbuilders. Just like a Viking longship, the cog had a clinker-built hull, a single mast and a square sail. But there were important differences. The cog had a straight keel, a cargo hold below deck and a hinged rudder for steering.

These ships were used by the great cities of northern Germany that made up the trading and commercial alliance known as the Hanseatic League. Because of this, they are often called Hansa cogs. They carried Europe's cargoes until the early fifteenth century. They also served as useful troop carriers in times of war, when their two "castles" acted as firing platforms for archers and crossbowmen.

SEA CASTLES

In 1340 English longbow archers helped to win the Battle of Sluys, a famous sea battle against the French fleet. They fired their dreaded "arrow storm" from the bow and stern castles of troop-filled cogs.

STEERING BY RUDDER

A cog's helmsman steered the ship by moving the tiller – a bar fixed to the top of the rudder. This was a far more efficient way to steer a ship than the steering oar, and was an important advance in ship design.

Rudder

BATTLE AT SEA

When they were used for fighting at sea, slow-sailing cogs did not ram each other. Instead, a cog would try to sail close to an enemy ship, sweeping its decks with arrow and crossbow fire. Then soldiers would try to board the other ship and capture it by hand-to-hand fighting. Sometimes the soldiers threw clouds of quicklime downwind, burning the defenders' eyes and blinding them – a savage but effective tactic. "Sea fights are always fiercer than fights on land," wrote Jean Froissart in the fourteenth century, "because retreat and flight are impossible. Every man must risk his life and hope for success, relying on his own personal bravery and skill."

A cog of 1350 was about 98ft. (30m) long and 23ft. (7m) across the beam. It could be handled by a crew of about ten.

Sail
Square mainsail on a single mast

Stern castle
Contained the poopdeck

Windlass
A winch for working weight-carrying cables

Hull
Clinker-built of overlapping planks

Cargo
Stored in the hold below the main deck

Deck beams
These were fixed through the sides of the ship

Bow castle

Bowsprit

THE WINDLASS

The stout, weight-carrying decks of the cog enabled it to be fitted with at least one windlass, or capstan – a winch used for hoisting heavy weights. It was usually mounted on the poopdeck in the stern or on the main deck. The windlass consisted of a cylindrical drum around which cables were wound. It was used to raise the heavy yard, or pole, that held the sail, or to lift cargo in and out of the hold.

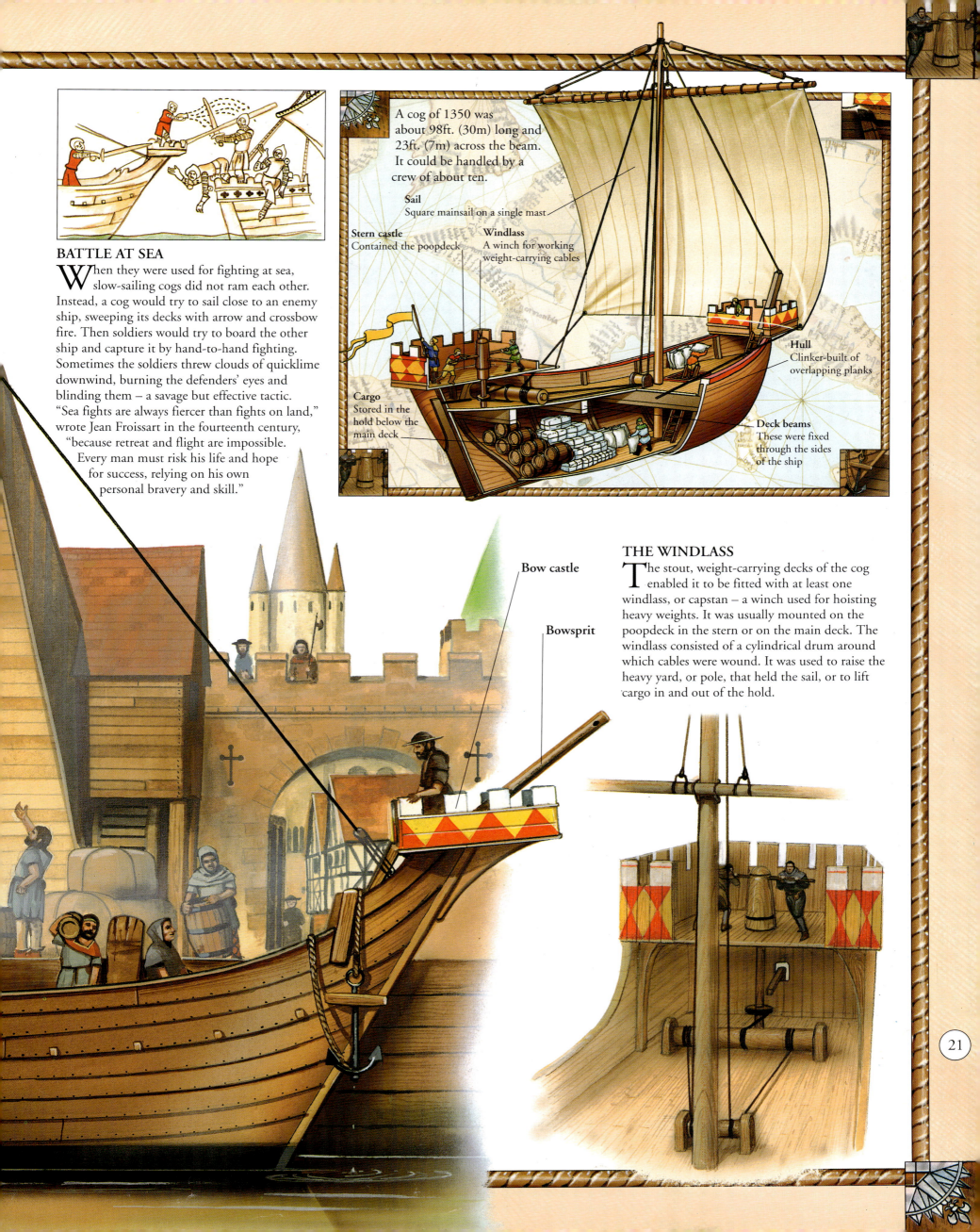

Caravel explorer

COAT OF ARMS

In 1493, Columbus was granted his own coat of arms by King Ferdinand and Queen Isabella of Spain.

PUNISHMENT AT SEA

A sailor who swore or answered back to officers was tied to the mast and gagged with a wooden bar, called a belaying pin, until his mouth bled.

NAVIGATION

The astrolabe, above, measured the height and position of the sun and stars. From this, the ship's position could be calculated. The traverse board, on the right, recorded the ship's course.

In the late 1400s European shipbuilders changed the design of the hull from the clinker-built style to the more streamlined caravel style. This meant laying the outer planks edge to edge over a strong framework built up from the keel. Using this method, Portuguese and Spanish caravels emerged as ships capable of making record-breaking voyages of discovery. The caravel opened sea routes to the Americas and the Far East. The *Niña*, illustrated below, was the favorite ship of Christopher Columbus, sailing on three of his four voyages to the New World. The caravel was a small ship, with a rounded bow and a square stern. It was the first European ship to carry the full "ship rig" of foremast, mainmast and mizzenmast. Bigger caravels had a fourth mast at the stern, called a "countermizzen."

Square mainsail

Square foresail

SHIP'S RATIONS

When fresh food ran out, food on board could be terrible, and was often made worse by being soaked with leaking bilge water. Weevils were in biscuits, maggots were in cheese, and the bacon and salt fish went rotten. Some food was cooked over a fire in an iron hearth.

Crow's nest

Lateen mizzen

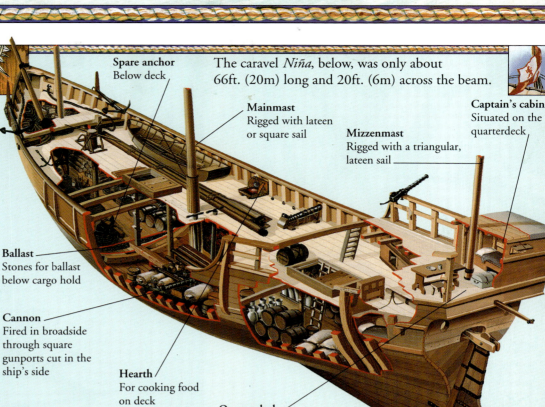

Spare anchor
Below deck

Mainmast
Rigged with lateen or square sail

Mizzenmast
Rigged with a triangular, lateen sail

Captain's cabin
Situated on the quarterdeck

The caravel *Niña*, below, was only about 66ft. (20m) long and 20ft. (6m) across the beam.

Ballast
Stones for ballast below cargo hold

Cannon
Fired in broadside through square gunports cut in the ship's side

Hearth
For cooking food on deck

Quarterdeck
Smaller, raised deck at the stern

ATLANTIC VOYAGES

The map below shows the routes taken by Columbus on his four Atlantic voyages. He sailed from Spain on the trade winds blowing west and south, and back on the North Atlantic winds.

1. **1st voyage** (1492–1493)
2. **2nd voyage** (1493–1494)
3. **3rd voyage** (1498–1500)
4. **4th voyage** (1502–1504)

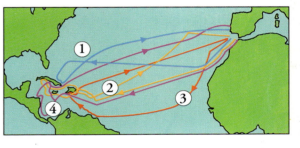

SAILS

Caravels usually carried triangular lateen sails. But for long voyages they were rigged with square sails to catch the following wind.

HULL DESIGN

The caravel's curved hull made it float high in the water. This was useful both in helping it cope with mid-ocean waves and for exploring treacherous shallows off unknown coasts.

Seventeenth-century

Warship

"Our condition is like to be very miserable. Our ships are extreme foul, winter drawing on, our victuals expiring, all stores failing, and our men falling sick through badness of drink and through eating their victuals boiled in salt water for two months' space."
Admiral Robert Blake to Oliver Cromwell, August, 1655

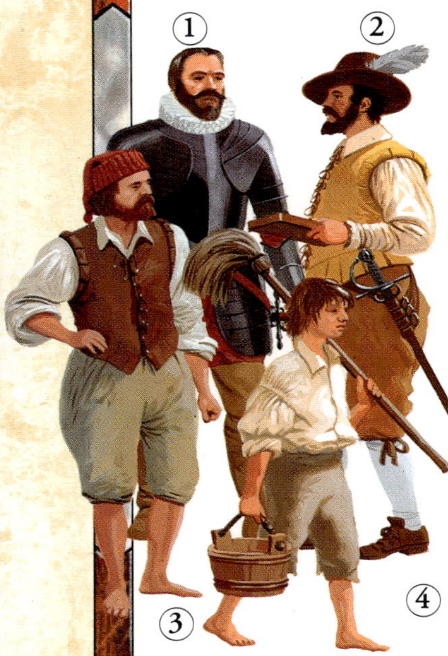

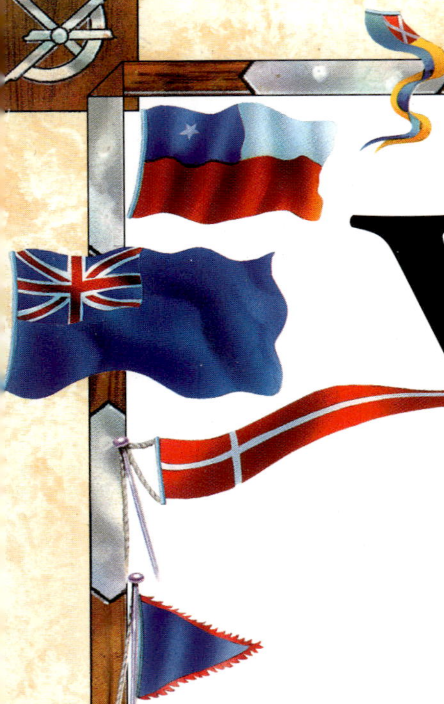

Between about 1570 and 1620, the galleon became the world's most powerful type of warship. It was armed with batteries of guns mounted to fire broadside, through ports cut in the ship's sides. Over the next 50 years the galleon developed into the two- or three-decked battleship of 100 guns or more, displacing over 2,000 tons and crewed by 800 or more sailors or troops. These great and beautiful ships were works of art, blazing with gold leaf and paint – but, as the above quotation, written in 1655, shows, life on board was tough.

FLAGS

Flags showed which country the ship belonged to and who commanded it. By the 1650s, flags were used to pass messages to other ships in the same fleet.

1
2
3
4

1. The captain
2. The ship's master
3. A seaman
4. The ship's boy

THE CREW

The captain was in overall control of the ship, but he often relied on the ship's master, a more experienced and trained sailor, who commanded the seamen. The ship also carried a fighting force of gunners and soldiers as well as craftsmen. The ship's boy was responsible for keeping the ship clean.

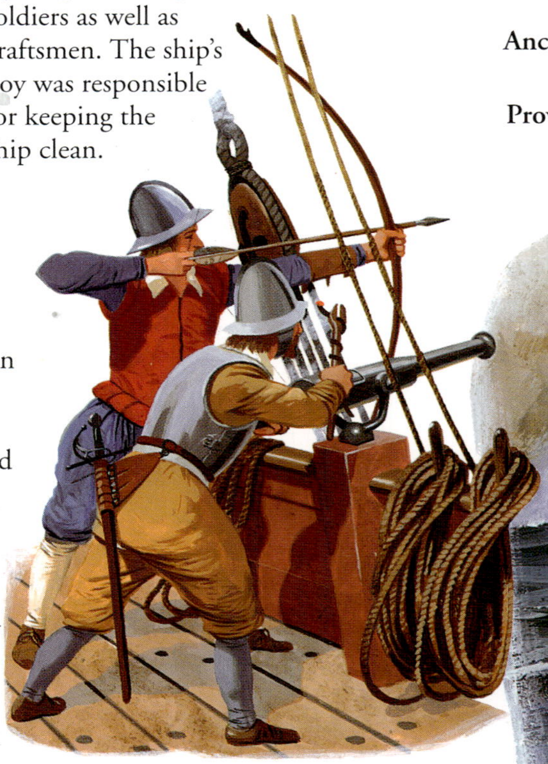

DECK FIGHTERS

As the ship approached an enemy vessel, lightweight swivel guns mounted on the rails sprayed its decks with lethal grape-shot. Some early warships carried a company of archers. Although they mainly fought on land, they could also defend their ship at sea if necessary.

Spritsail
Bowsprit
Beakhead
Anchor
Prow

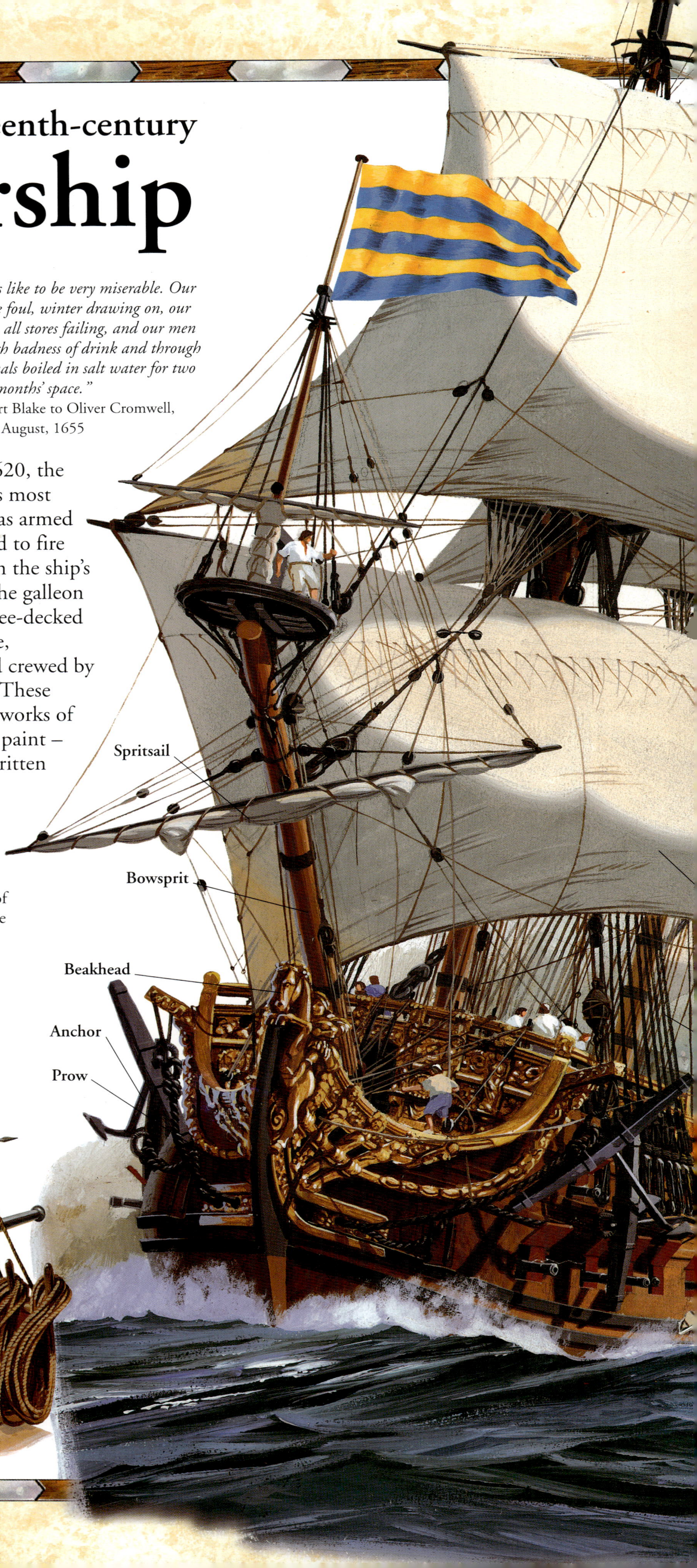

AT THE MASTHEAD

Where the sections of the masts joined, round platforms called "tops" helped the sailors work aloft. They also served as lookout posts and carried sharp-shooters.

Main yardarm
A horizontal spar from which the largest sail on the main mast hung

Whipstaff
A vertical lever connected to the rudder for steering the ship

Forecastle
A raised section at the ship's bow housing the crew's living quarters

Gun ports
Holes cut in the hull for guns to fire through

Galley
Area where food was prepared, generally by boiling

A seventeenth-century warship was about 131ft. (40m) long, with a keel 98ft. (30m) long, and a beam (width) of 36ft. (11m). It carried a crew of about 300 sailors and 100 soldiers, and was armed with about 40 guns.

Fore topsail

Main topsail

Forecourse

Mainshroud

BEAUTY AND FIRE-POWER

A big royal flagship like *Kronan* was built to show the wealth and power of the king or state. It carried rich carvings outside, even around the gun ports. The English *Sovereign of the Seas*, launched in 1637, was decorated with so much gold leaf that its enemies called it "Golden Devil." But if properly looked after they served for many more years than modern warships.

AT THE HELM

A galleon was steered by means of a lever called the whipstaff operated by the ship's helmsman. As the whipstaff was below deck, the helmsman could not see where the ship was going. He had to follow instructions shouted down through a hatch to him by an officer on deck. When the captain ordered a change of course, the helmsman pushed the whipstaff to one side, which swung the ship's rudder around and turned the ship.

SERVING THE GUNS

The ship's value in battle depended on how fast the guns could be reloaded and fired. After each shot the gun had to be sponged clean of fragments that were still burning, reloaded with a rammed-in powder charge and shot, then run out again. Ten or more men were needed to crew each of the heaviest guns.

Steamship

By the 1830s, sailing ships were being fitted with steam engines for extra power on ocean voyages, but the amount of coal they could carry was small. After his steamships the *Great Western* and the *Great Britain*, launched in 1837 and 1843, the British engineer Isambard Kingdom Brunel planned an even bigger iron ship. This was the *Great Eastern*, shown below, which was built to carry enough coal to steam to India and Australia and was launched in 1858.

Driven by sail, paddlewheels and a stern propeller, this giant steamship was designed to carry 4,000 passengers and 6,000 tons of cargo. It was the biggest ship built before the 1890s, but it was dogged by problems and was a failure as a passenger ship. The *Great Eastern* laid the first successful Atlantic telegraph cable in 1866, but was scrapped in 1888.

GIANT PADDLES

The *Great Eastern*'s two huge paddlewheels were each 56ft. (17m) in diameter. They added almost 36ft. (11m) to the overall width of the ship and had an effect similar to giant brakes, which ruined its abilities as a sailing ship.

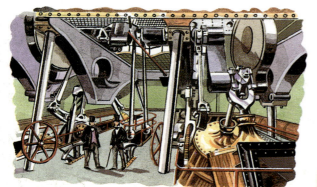

PUSH-PULL ENGINES

Each of the *Great Eastern*'s giant paddlewheels was driven by a huge two-cylinder engine. The oscillating engines pushed and pulled the paddlewheel crankshafts around in great circles. With an enormous piston and piston rod, each cylinder weighed nearly 30 tons. These massive engines, with their unguarded, whirling cranks and couplings, were at once cumbersome, dangerous and deafening.

Starboard paddlewheel

Lifeboat

PROPELLER

The massive four-bladed screw propeller at the stern was over 23ft. (7m) across and weighed over 36 tons. It was driven from a separate engine room by a row of four cylinders, each of which, if required, could work independently of the others.

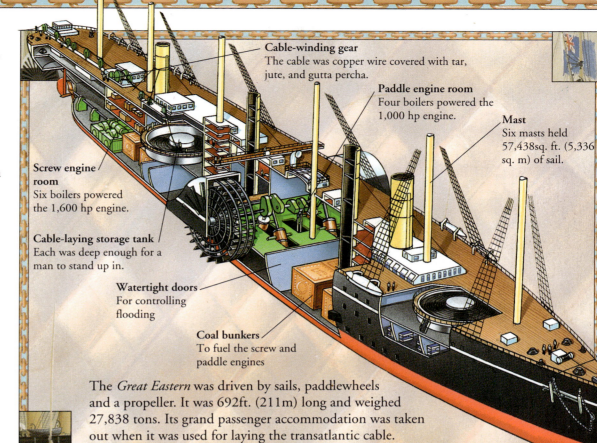

Cable-winding gear
The cable was copper wire covered with tar, jute, and gutta percha.

Paddle engine room
Four boilers powered the 1,000 hp engine.

Mast
Six masts held 57,438sq. ft. (5,336 sq. m) of sail.

Screw engine room
Six boilers powered the 1,600 hp engine.

Cable-laying storage tank
Each was deep enough for a man to stand up in.

Watertight doors
For controlling flooding

Coal bunkers
To fuel the screw and paddle engines

The *Great Eastern* was driven by sails, paddlewheels and a propeller. It was 692ft. (211m) long and weighed 27,838 tons. Its grand passenger accommodation was taken out when it was used for laying the transatlantic cable.

Iron-tube mast

Sails furled to yards

Wire rigging

LAYING CABLE

The *Great Eastern* was the only ship in the world big enough to carry enough cable (2,499mi. [4,022 km], weighing 4,673 tons) to stretch across the Atlantic seabed from Ireland to Newfoundland. The task was achieved in July, 1866.

Ironclad

"Our hope, our one chance, is the Monitor.*"*
Gideon Welles,
United States Navy Secretary, 1862

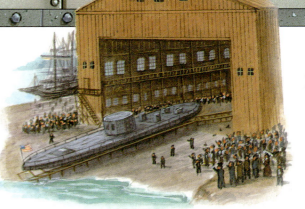

STEEL SHOT

Steel shot were needed to pierce armor plate. The *Merrimack* went into battle before hers were ready, and so she fired explosive shells instead. The *Monitor*'s shot were fired with reduced powder charges, and most bounced off the *Merrimack*'s sloping armor.

By the late 1830s, wooden sailing ships faced a new threat – rifled cannon firing explosive shells instead of solid shot. Wooden ships simply could not withstand this shellfire. Metal armor was needed, and so by 1860 the French and British navies had built warships protected by iron plates – "ironclads." The first was France's *Gloire,* a wooden steam frigate with an iron "belt" above the waterline, followed by Britain's all-iron *Warrior.* During the American Civil War (1861-1865), steam-powered ironclads met in battle for the first time. The South built the *Merrimack,* and the North replied by building the *Monitor,* shown below, with a rotating armored turret. Conditions inside the ships would have been extremely hot. They fought in 1862 in Virginia, blasting each other at close range for over two hours. Neither was able to pierce the armor of the other and the battle ended in stalemate. A new age in naval warfare had begun.

LAUNCH

The *Monitor* took only four months to build, and was ready for launch in January 1862. Many experts doubted that she would even float. To prove them wrong, the ship's designer, John Ericsson, stood on deck during the *Monitor*'s successful launch in New York.

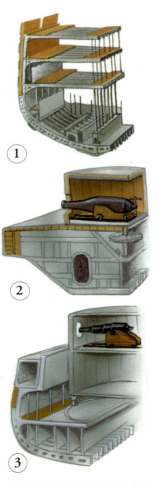

IRONCLAD HULLS

The *Warrior* (1861) had a hull with an armored belt lined on the inside with teak wood (1). The *Monitor* (1862) had a flat hull which lay low in the water to give little for enemy ships to fire at (2). The *Buffel* (1868) had a stronger hull with a rounded bottom to enable it to cope with the seas (3).

Smoke stack

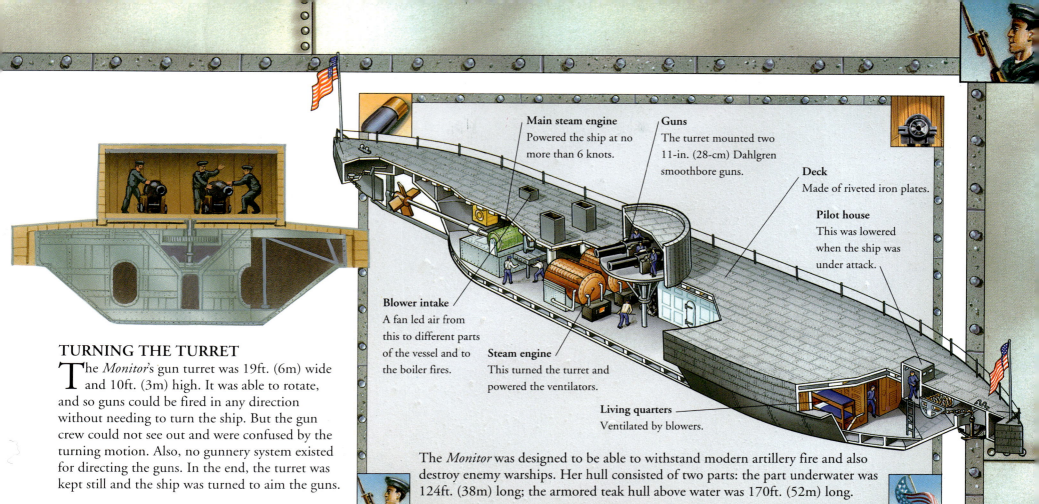

Main steam engine
Powered the ship at no
more than 6 knots.

Guns
The turret mounted two
11-in. (28-cm) Dahlgren
smoothbore guns.

Deck
Made of riveted iron plates.

Pilot house
This was lowered
when the ship was
under attack.

Blower intake
A fan led air from
this to different parts
of the vessel and to
the boiler fires.

Steam engine
This turned the turret and
powered the ventilators.

Living quarters
Ventilated by blowers.

The *Monitor* was designed to be able to withstand modern artillery fire and also
destroy enemy warships. Her hull consisted of two parts: the part underwater was
124ft. (38m) long; the armored teak hull above water was 170ft. (52m) long.

TURNING THE TURRET

The *Monitor*'s gun turret was 19ft. (6m) wide
and 10ft. (3m) high. It was able to rotate,
and so guns could be fired in any direction
without needing to turn the ship. But the gun
crew could not see out and were confused by the
turning motion. Also, no gunnery system existed
for directing the guns. In the end, the turret was
kept still and the ship was turned to aim the guns.

Gun turret

Guard rail

FIRING THE GUNS

The *Monitor*'s two 132-lb. (60-kg)guns had a bore 11in. (28 cm) in
diameter. They could fire a shot over a mile (2km). However, they
had not been tested at full power before the 1862 battle. The ship's
gunners were ordered to use half-strength charges. The *Merrimack* had ten
guns, with four on each side and one each at bow and stern. The biggest
danger to both crews was being in contact with the armor plating when
an enemy shot struck. The impact from it could knock a man senseless.

RIVETING

The ironclad's plates were riveted together,
which was a new method of shipbuilding.
Red-hot rivets were pushed through holes drilled
in the plates, then hammered flat. The *Monitor*'s
turret had eight riveted layers of 1-in. (2.5-cm)
iron plate.

Sailing Clipper

"Her only motive-power was the ocean wind. Her passage and her very hope of survival lay in the skills of her master and the strong, able arms of her seamen. Her "engines" were a gentle tracery of masts and yards and maze of rigging."
Alan Villiers, The *Cutty Sark*

Clippers were the fastest wind-driven merchant ships ever built. They carried cargoes over long distances in the shortest possible time, "clipping" days off the sailing time of other ships. Clippers sailed from China to London carrying tea, and from Australia to London carrying wool. They also carried emigrants to California around Cape Horn. Their heyday was from 1840 to 1880, at which time the new steamships could not match their speed. One of the most famous clipper ships is the *Cutty Sark*, shown below. She sailed her maiden voyage in February 1870, and was intended to be the fastest ship in the China tea race.

Clipper hulls were extremely narrow, slicing through the sea under as much sail as possible. But their cargoes and passenger numbers were small, and they were reliant on the wind. Larger, faster steamers were bound to take over in the end.

FIGUREHEAD

Sailing ships often had figureheads on their bow which reflected the name of the ship. The figurehead on the *Cutty Sark* was of a woman wearing a cutty sark, which was a linen shirt.

Figurehead

CATCHING THE WIND

The *Cutty Sark* had 34 sails, providing a sail area of 31,991sq. yds. (2,972sq. m). This gave it a maximum speed of just over 17 knots. The large sail area enabled clippers to maximize the power of the wind. The basic sails on all three masts were: 1. Course; 2. Lower topsail; 3. Upper topsail; 4. Top gallant; 5. Royal; 6. Skysail.

30

WOOL TRADE

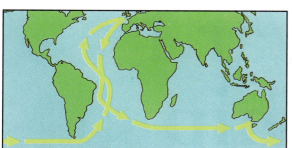

Clippers used the winds known as the "Roaring Forties" to sail to Australia via the Cape of Good Hope, just below southern Africa, returning eastward around Cape Horn, which is just below South America.

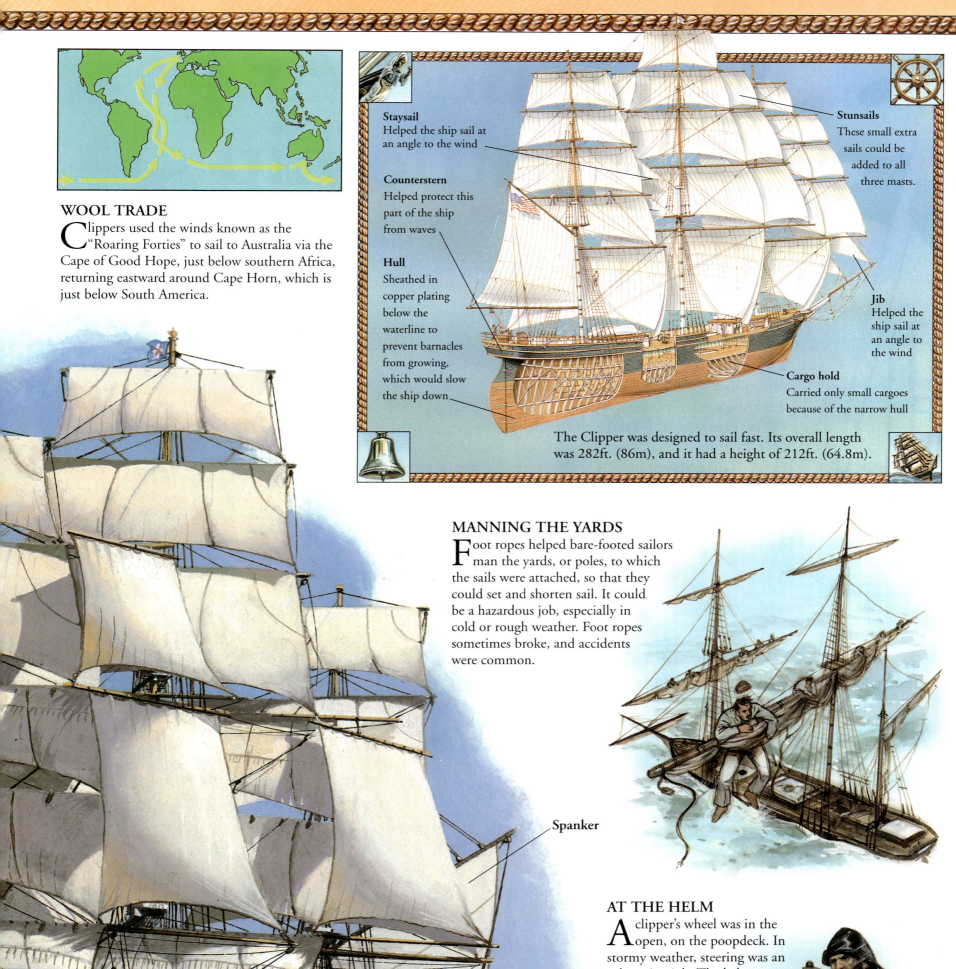

Staysail
Helped the ship sail at an angle to the wind

Counterstern
Helped protect this part of the ship from waves

Hull
Sheathed in copper plating below the waterline to prevent barnacles from growing, which would slow the ship down

Stunsails
These small extra sails could be added to all three masts.

Jib
Helped the ship sail at an angle to the wind

Cargo hold
Carried only small cargoes because of the narrow hull

The Clipper was designed to sail fast. Its overall length was 282ft. (86m), and it had a height of 212ft. (64.8m).

MANNING THE YARDS

Foot ropes helped bare-footed sailors man the yards, or poles, to which the sails were attached, so that they could set and shorten sail. It could be a hazardous job, especially in cold or rough weather. Foot ropes sometimes broke, and accidents were common.

Spanker

AT THE HELM

A clipper's wheel was in the open, on the poopdeck. In stormy weather, steering was an exhausting job. The helmsman had to watch out for every shift in the wind, to prevent damage to the sails.

31

World War I battleship

"As the German ships one after another emerged from the mist, all the British battleships whose range was clear opened a terrific fire upon them. The German van, the formidable Königs, saw the whole horizon as far as the eye could reach alive with flashes. The concussion of the shell storm broke upon the German vessels."
Winston Churchill, *The World Crisis*

By the 1880s, improvements in steam engines meant that warships no longer needed masts and sails. Battleships were large, heavily armored steamships with powerful, long-range guns. These were breech-loading guns, which meant that shells were loaded into the breech behind the barrel. This allowed gun crews to load and fire from inside an armored turret.

By 1900 the biggest danger to the new battleships was powered torpedoes, fired from fast boats. Then, in 1906, came Britain's *Dreadnought* battleship, which carried ten heavy guns and could steam faster than any other battleship afloat. Other navies began to build similar ships, and at the beginning of World War I, Britain had 20 "Dreadnoughts" to Germany's 14. The two battleship fleets fought only once, at the Battle of Jutland in 1916, and the result was indecisive. The British fleet lost more men and a heavier tonnage of ships, while the smaller German fleet fled to base and never risked another battle.

FLAG SIGNALS

In World War I, flags were still hoisted to act as signals. Flag signals were used to communicate between battleships and to direct fleet movements. Each flag stood for a letter or a code word.

LOADING THE GUNS

Shells and cordite charges were hoisted to gun turrets from the ammunition magazine below the waterline. Two men loaded the gun, while two more held the next shell and charge ready. All loaders wore long gloves and hoods to protect their skin from the scorching flash when the gun was fired. *Dreadnought* could fire an eight-gun salvo. This meant that eight of its ten big guns could fire in the same direction at the same time.

MUSKETRY DRILL

Sailors still had to practice firing a rifle, and so there was regular musketry drill. The long range of the battleships' big guns made it impossible for ships to get close enough to each other to use rifles, but sailors had to be ready to fight on shore if necessary.

Boom for anti-torpedo net   Light 119-lb. (54-kg) gun

Radio aerial

WIRELESS

Radio communication, or wireless as it was known, was the latest technology in World War I. It made it possible for admiralties and governments to communicate with their fleets at sea, and to listen to the enemy's radio messages. To begin with they used Morse Code, with its alphabet of dots and dashes, but later, voice communications systems were developed.

Union Jack
Flown on the jack staff

Cleaver bow
Designed for ramming enemy ships

Anti-torpedo net
Fixed to steel supports called booms

Ensign staff
Flew Ensign

Turbine engine
Pushed steam against thousands of blades mounted on shafts, which turned the propellers

Coal bunker
Provided fuel for the steam turbine engines

Dreadnought was armed with ten 12-in. (30.5-cm) guns. It was 525ft. (160m) long, displaced 21,000 tons, had a crew of 862, and its heaviest armor was 11in. (28cm) thick.

STOKING THE BOILERS

Although the powerful new turbine engine provided the increased speeds of World War I dreadnoughts, the boilers were still fired by coal. The biggest battleships carried 3,650 tons or more, stored in bunkers down the sides of the ship. The engine-room stokers had an exhausting and filthy job, not only keeping the boilers fired but laboring in the bunkers to keep the coal evenly stowed so the ship remained stable in the water. "Coaling ship," or loading with coal, covered the whole ship with grit and black dust.

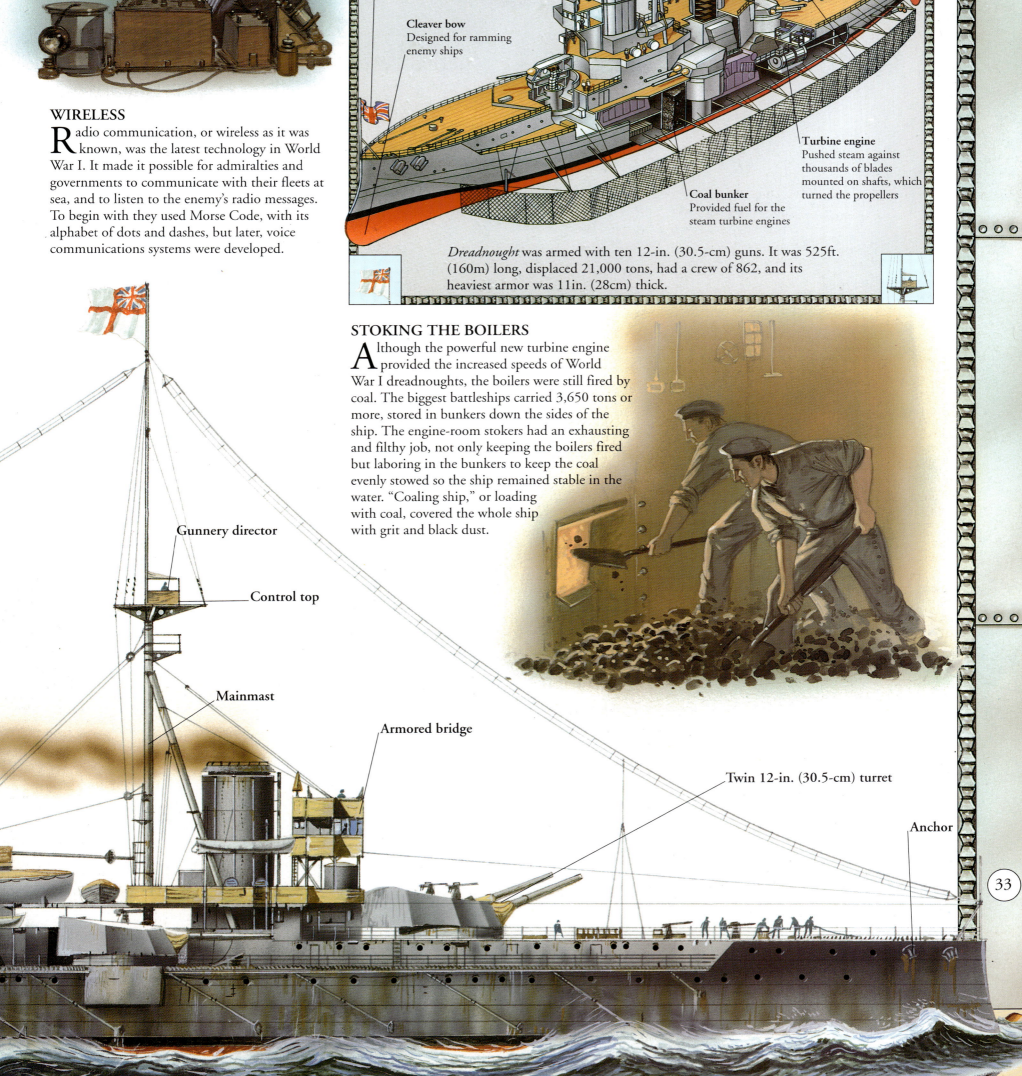

Gunnery director

Control top

Mainmast

Armored bridge

Twin 12-in. (30.5-cm) turret

Anchor

L 1930s Luxury liner

"Perhaps the best service the world has ever known was that given in the trans-Atlantic luxury liners in the '20s and '30s. Menus ten pages long, food from every quarter of the globe, masterpieces of art hanging on the bulkheads, orchestras and gymnasiums and swimming baths . . ."
C.S. Forester, *The Ship*

SHIP-TO-SHORE STREAMERS

The gaiety and excitement of departure was helped by the passengers' custom of throwing paper streamers from the ship to the dock, as symbols of breaking ties with the land.

STORES FOR A SINGLE CROSSING

The range of food, drink, and stores shipped by the *Queen Mary* for a single Atlantic crossing – enough for 1,432 first class, 1,510 second class, and 1,058 third class passengers – is shown below, together with some of the fixed items used in the building of the ship.

From the 1880s until the coming of cheap air travel in the 1960s, the quickest and most comfortable way of crossing the Atlantic was by passenger liner. The big liners of Europe and America competed for the "Blue Riband of the Atlantic," awarded for the quickest crossing. The luxury,

comfort and service provided for first class passengers was the best in the world. Even for the poorest passengers in the third class or steerage, seeking a new life in America, their liner cabins were usually the finest housing they had ever known. In the 1930s, France's *Normandie* and Britain's *Queen Mary* were the biggest, fastest ships ever to have been built.

20 tons meat		100,000 pieces china and glass	
20 tons fish		21,000 tablecloths	
3,968lb. (1,800kg) tea and coffee		5,600 blankets	
9,920lb. (4,500kg) sugar		31,000 pillowcases	
70,000 eggs		92,000 napkins	
3,960gal. (18,000l) milk		210,000 towels	
3 tons butter		6mi. (10km) carpet	
1,984lb. (900kg) cheese		30,000 light bulbs	
10,000 bottles wine		69,952gal. (318,000l) paint	
4,400gal. (20,000l) beer		10 million rivets	
20,000 packs cigarettes		3,977mi. (6,400km) electric cable	
5,000 cigars		4,000 passengers	
39,682lb. (18,000kg) veg		1,200 crew	
5,000 bottles spirits		13mi. (21km) fabrics	

Crow's nest

Fore funnel

Bridge

Midship funnel

Aft funnel

Lifeboats

QUEEN MARY

34

FROM KEEL TO FUNNEL

From keel to funnel-tops, the *Queen Mary* would have towered 33ft. (10m) higher than the Statue of Liberty's upraised torch, if the two giant structures could have been placed side by side.

First class smoking room
Each class of passenger had its own smoking room, swimming pool, bars and dining room.

Engine room
The engines had a total of 200,000 hp. They were in separate rooms to prevent excessive vibration.

Main lounge
For first class passengers only

Wireless room
For communicating with other ships and ports

Boiler rooms
Where water was turned into steam for the furnaces

Sport's deck
Passengers usually played tennis.

Port-side lifeboats
Each lifeboat could carry 145 people.

Cargo hold
The ship's stores were kept here.

Displacing 82,000 tons, the *Queen Mary* was the biggest floating structure ever built. It was 1,017ft. (310m) long and 118ft. (36m) across the beam.

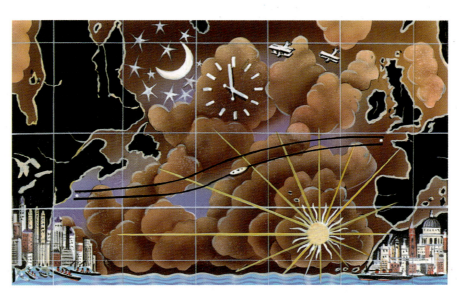

SPANNING THE ATLANTIC

This enormous map and clock were displayed on the wall of the *Queen Mary*'s main dining hall. With New York and London on opposite sides of the North Atlantic, it featured a moving model which showed the ship's position throughout the voyage.

SOCIAL LIFE

A seat at the captain's table was regarded as an honor by the richest and most famous passengers. They were also entertained with dances, parties and sporting activities. With the exception of France's *Normandie*, which it was built to match, *Queen Mary* offered passengers more luxurious features than any liner that had ever been built.

World War II submarine

"The key to German power at sea lies below the surface. Give us submarines and we shall have the teeth to attack."
Grand-Admiral Raeder to Adolf Hitler, 1934

In World War I, submarines had shown themselves to be a deadly new type of underwater warship. By the start of World War II (1939–1945), the world's leading navies had all built submarine fleets. Germany had its U-boats. The German *U-Boot* is short for *Unterseeboot*, meaning literally "undersea boat." U-boats came close to winning the Battle of the Atlantic between 1940 and 1943, when they sank thousands of tons of allied shipping thus preventing vital supplies from reaching Britain.

The Type VII U-boat played a leading role in the Atlantic battle. It was powered by diesel engines on the surface and by an electric motor when submerged. The U-boat shown below carried 14 torpedoes, fired from four tubes in the bow and one in the stern. There was also a 3-in. (8.8-cm) gun on the deck for surface fighting.

UP PERISCOPE!

The periscope was raised to give the captain a 360° view from under water. Red lighting in the submarine helped him to see more clearly through the periscope.

Mooring cleat

DIVING AND SURFACING

Submarines dive by flooding the ballast tanks that surround the inner hull where the crew live and work. To surface again, the seawater is forced back out of the ballast tanks by compressed air.

1. Submarine on the surface: top vents are shut, and outer ballast tanks full of air, giving the submarine buoyancy.

2. Submarine diving: top vents and bottom vents are open, seawater is flooding into outer ballast tanks and driving air out through vents.

3. Submarine surfacing: top vents are shut again, and compressed air is forcing seawater out of outer ballast tanks.

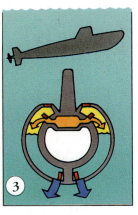

The Type VII U-boat was 220ft. (67m) long and had a crew of 44 submariners. It could travel at 17 knots on the surface and 7 knots under water.

Periscope
Raised when the U-boat was just below the surface of the water

Torpedo-tube caps
Outer caps closed the torpedo tubes.

Watertight doors
Prevented the whole vessel from flooding

Ballast tanks
Surrounded the inner hull

Engines
Powerful diesel engines drove the U-boat at 17 knots on the surface.

Batteries
For the electric motor

Torpedoes
These were fired into the sea by compressed air.

Venting holes
In outer casing, for filling and emptying ballast tanks

LIFE ON BOARD

There was little room on a U-boat. Folding bunks behind the bow tubes could only be used when the spare torpedoes had been fired and the submarine was heading back to port. With no water for washing, submariners tended to suffer from boils and other skin complaints. It was also damp, which often made food turn moldy.

3-in. (8.8-cm) deck gun

Conning tower

HUNTING SUBMARINES

Sonar – from "SOund NAvigation and Ranging" – was used by surface ships to detect submarines. A sound pulse or "ping" hit an object, and sent back an echo. The submarine crew heard the "ping" as a metallic tapping. The enemy ship dropped depth charges which exploded under water, forcing the submarine to surface and surrender, or blowing it apart.

PROPELLERS

Most submarines were driven by two propellers. Submarines carried a hydrophone that could detect the sounds of other propellers from surface ships or other submarines.

LOADING THE TUBES

Torpedo operators had an exhausting job when the time came to reload. The torpedo was lowered onto guide rails – a difficult and dangerous task if the submarine was rolling. Then it was hauled into the tube. The torpedo was launched into the sea with a blast of compressed air. As the torpedo shot forward, its own engine started up. This carried it to the target ship.

Aircraft carrier

"The fleet carrier . . . can unleash a greater variety of lethal weapons with greater destructive power . . . than any man-of-war in history."
Admiral of the fleet, Lord Hill-Norton

Air search radar scanner

Lifeboat

The first aircraft carriers were built at the end of World War I (1914–1918); too late to play an active part in that conflict. In World War II (1939–1945) they replaced the battleship as the most important heavy warship.

The air group (aircraft) on board a carrier includes fighters to shoot down enemy aircraft, and strike aircraft to attack enemy ships and land targets with bombs, torpedoes, and rockets. Modern carriers are the biggest and most complex warships ever built. The largest carriers are floating air bases, built to carry all the fuel, weapons and spares to keep their air groups flying and fighting. Nuclear-powered carriers can travel for over one million miles (2 million km) without refueling.

SHIP'S CREW

In addition to the captain, officers and seamen, half the crew are aviation personnel. A landing signals officer guides pilots down to a safe landing while fire crews stand by.
1. Captain
2. Landing Signals Officer (LSO)
3. Pilot
4. Fire crew
5. Officer

DEVELOPMENT OF THE CARRIER

Experiments with separate flying-off and landing-on decks proved too dangerous, so carriers were given single flight decks extending from bow to stern. The superstructure with the bridge and command center were placed on the starboard side of the flight deck.

Landing Signals Officer control station

LIFE ON BOARD

The largest carriers are crewed by up to 6,000 men, who have to be fed three times a day, so a carrier's kitchens rarely close. The crew work hard but they also have to be entertained when they are off duty. Some carriers have shops, a cinema, satellite television and even their own television station on board broadcasting to the crew.

TAKEOFF

By 1945, the dawn of the jet age, carrier planes were becoming so big and heavy that their engines could not launch them fast enough. They needed the extra punch of a catapult driven by steam from the ship's boilers. Each plane is hitched to it by a sling which falls away once the plane is airborne.

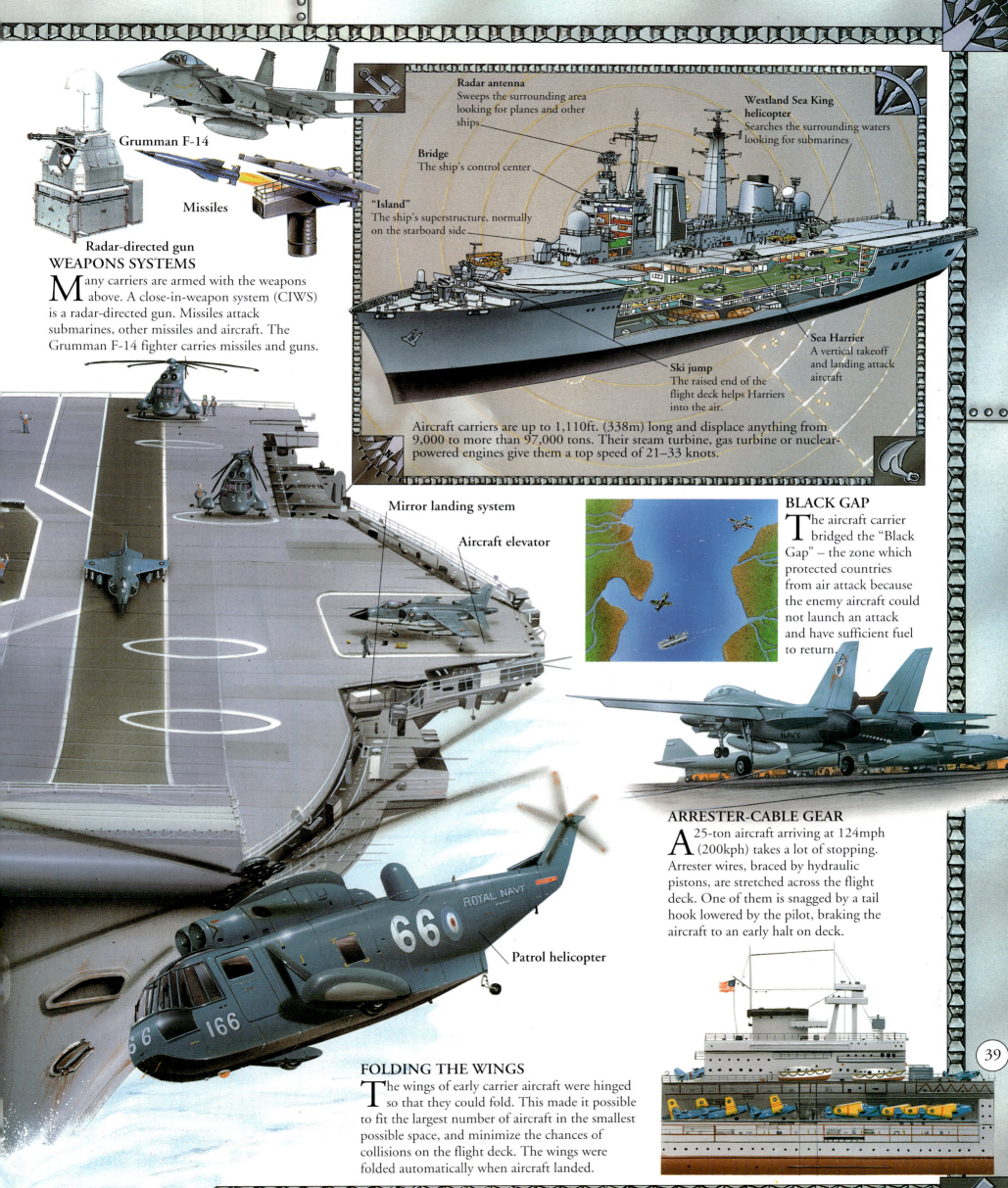

WEAPONS SYSTEMS

Grumman F-14

Missiles

Radar-directed gun

Many carriers are armed with the weapons above. A close-in-weapon system (CIWS) is a radar-directed gun. Missiles attack submarines, other missiles and aircraft. The Grumman F-14 fighter carries missiles and guns.

Radar antenna
Sweeps the surrounding area looking for planes and other ships

Bridge
The ship's control center

"Island"
The ship's superstructure, normally on the starboard side

Westland Sea King helicopter
Searches the surrounding waters looking for submarines

Sea Harrier
A vertical takeoff and landing attack aircraft

Ski jump
The raised end of the flight deck helps Harriers into the air.

Aircraft carriers are up to 1,110ft. (338m) long and displace anything from 9,000 to more than 97,000 tons. Their steam turbine, gas turbine or nuclear-powered engines give them a top speed of 21–33 knots.

Mirror landing system

Aircraft elevator

BLACK GAP

The aircraft carrier bridged the "Black Gap" – the zone which protected countries from air attack because the enemy aircraft could not launch an attack and have sufficient fuel to return.

Patrol helicopter

ARRESTER-CABLE GEAR

A 25-ton aircraft arriving at 124mph (200kph) takes a lot of stopping. Arrester wires, braced by hydraulic pistons, are stretched across the flight deck. One of them is snagged by a tail hook lowered by the pilot, braking the aircraft to an early halt on deck.

FOLDING THE WINGS

The wings of early carrier aircraft were hinged so that they could fold. This made it possible to fit the largest number of aircraft in the smallest possible space, and minimize the chances of collisions on the flight deck. The wings were folded automatically when aircraft landed.

39

Supertanker

"The most catastrophic spill out of the pipeline would be 60,000 barrels of oil. A 167,000-ton tanker carries about one million barrels."
Charles Champion, Alaska pipeline coordinator, 1978

Crude oil, as pumped from the ground, is a vital energy source. Every developed country in the world depends on oil. It is used as fuel in power stations for generating electricity, and refined to make gasoline and diesel fuels for all sorts of vehicles.

Since the 1960s, the world's demand for oil has produced the most gigantic ships ever built: supertankers. If a supertanker can carry over 200,000 tons of crude oil, people in the industry call it a VLCC, a "very large crude carrier." And if it is enormous enough to carry over 300,000 tons – that's equivalent to nearly two million barrels of oil – then they call it a ULCC, an "ultra-large crude carrier."

At 1,240ft. (378m) long and 164ft. (50m) wide, the supertanker *Globtik Tokyo* is certainly ultra-large. The ship's bridge, crew quarters and engines are all located in the stern, leaving nine-tenths of the ship to be taken up by oil container tanks.

Lifeboat   Funnel   Bridge

GLOBTIK TO

CARGO STOWAGE

No other form of merchant ship is so devoted to cargo stowage as the tanker. Nine-tenths of a tanker consists of the carefully separated tanks holding the oil. A mere one-tenth of the ship holds the engines, crew accommodation, bridge and controls.

OIL SPILL

Supertanker accidents cause environmental ruin when the poisonous cargo floods into the sea. In 1989 an oil spill from the *Exxon Valdez* polluted 1,056mi. (1,700km) of coastline in Alaska. It spilled 11 million gallons of oil, destroying local wildlife.

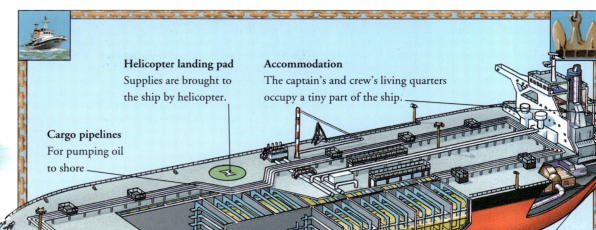

FLOATING GIANTS

A supertanker simply dwarfs a big car ferry. Many supertankers are as long as four soccer pitches! The biggest, the *Jahre Viking*, is 1,591ft. (485m) long, 226ft. (69m) wide and weighs 565,000 tons. Not surprisingly, it is the world's largest ship.

Helicopter landing pad
Supplies are brought to the ship by helicopter.

Accommodation
The captain's and crew's living quarters occupy a tiny part of the ship.

Cargo pipelines
For pumping oil to shore

Propeller
The five-blade screw propeller has a diameter of 30ft. (9m).

Vertical and horizontal frames
Separate the oil into small compartments to prevent massive surging as the ship pitches and rolls

The ULCC *Esso Atlantic* (1977) is 1,332ft. (406m) long and displaces 517,144 tons. Its 45,000 hp steam-turbine powerplant is as high as a 16-story building.

HIGH-TECH SAILING

Supertanker captains need great skill to pilot their huge vessels. Tankers have a wide turning circle and respond slowly to a change of course. Even at the low speed of eight knots, they need one mile (2km) or more to stop. On-board computers help navigation and reduce the risk of collision with other smaller ships.

OFFSHORE PIPELINES

A fully laden supertanker lies too deep in the water – 72ft. (22m) or more – to enter an ordinary harbor. VLCCs and ULCCs use deep-water anchorages and unload their oil by pumping it through miles of pipeline to "tank farms" on shore.

Destroyer

"After their Sea Dart SAM failed to fire, Glasgow held steady while we fought the battle. Two Sea Wolf SAMs were fired, and they took out the first two aircraft."
Captain John Coward, Falkland Islands, 1982

A hundred years ago, the first destroyers were light, fast warships designed to protect a fleet from torpedo attack. Then they were given tubes to allow them to make torpedo attacks themselves. Modern destroyers still have this dual role of defense and attack, but today their most important weapons are missiles. SSMs (surface-to-surface missiles) can attack other ships, and SAMs (surface-to-air missiles) can destroy aircraft.

Since World War II, destroyers have also carried sonar and antisubmarine weapons. Modern destroyers carry helicopters to widen the search for submarines. A helicopter moves rapidly across the sea, using its sonar to detect enemy submarines. It uses its own antisubmarine weapons to attack the submarines. A destroyer like the French *Tourville*, shown below, has enormous fire-power and is very fast. It is armed with two 4-in. (10-cm) guns, Exocet SSMs, Crotale SAMs and Malafon hunting torpedoes. The ship's top speed is 34 knots.

RADAR

Modern destroyers have separate radar systems for detecting other ships and aircraft, for guiding missiles, and for navigating the ship.

Radar array

SAM launcher

Helicopter landing pad

MISSILE LAUNCH

Missiles are usually mounted in groups for rapid firing. French Crotale SAMs are mounted in two groups of four missiles.

AIR ATTACK RED!

Warship crews are not kept at battle stations all the time, but work at different levels of readiness. The most urgent level is "Air attack red." This means that an enemy missile or bomb attack might be only minutes or even seconds away. Anti-flash hoods and gloves reduce the risk of burns.

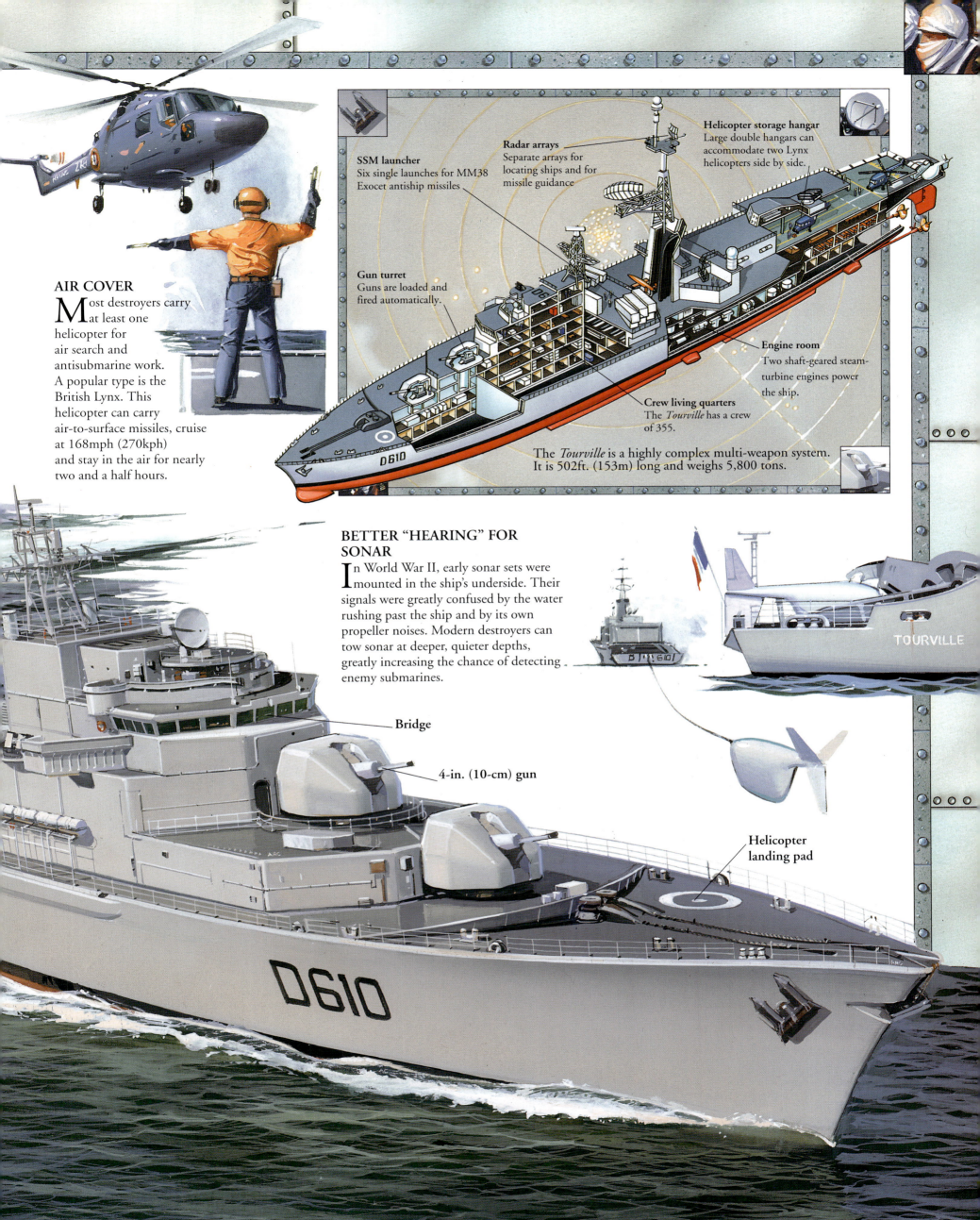

AIR COVER

Most destroyers carry at least one helicopter for air search and antisubmarine work. A popular type is the British Lynx. This helicopter can carry air-to-surface missiles, cruise at 168mph (270kph) and stay in the air for nearly two and a half hours.

SSM launcher
Six single launches for MM38 Exocet antiship missiles

Radar arrays
Separate arrays for locating ships and for missile guidance

Helicopter storage hangar
Large double hangars can accommodate two Lynx helicopters side by side.

Gun turret
Guns are loaded and fired automatically.

Engine room
Two shaft-geared steam-turbine engines power the ship.

Crew living quarters
The *Tourville* has a crew of 355.

The *Tourville* is a highly complex multi-weapon system. It is 502ft. (153m) long and weighs 5,800 tons.

BETTER "HEARING" FOR SONAR

In World War II, early sonar sets were mounted in the ship's underside. Their signals were greatly confused by the water rushing past the ship and by its own propeller noises. Modern destroyers can tow sonar at deeper, quieter depths, greatly increasing the chance of detecting enemy submarines.

Bridge

4-in. (10-cm) gun

Helicopter landing pad

TOURVILLE

D610

High-speed ferry

Over the past ten years, one of the most exciting new ship types to enter service has been the high-speed multi-hull ferry. The advantage of the multi-hull ship is that it is both light and stable, less likely to roll than a single-hulled ship and therefore more comfortable for passengers. A multi-hull, such as the *Hoverspeed Great Britain*, takes advantage of the fact that the less a hull is in contact with the water, the faster it will move through it. The *Hoverspeed Great Britain* features the wave-slicing bows of the old clipper sailing ship, and the lines of a modern powerboat, for extra speed. Unlike other craft, multi-hulls are driven by water-jet nozzles, two in each hull. Instead of having a rudder for steering, they are steered by pivoting the ends of the nozzles.

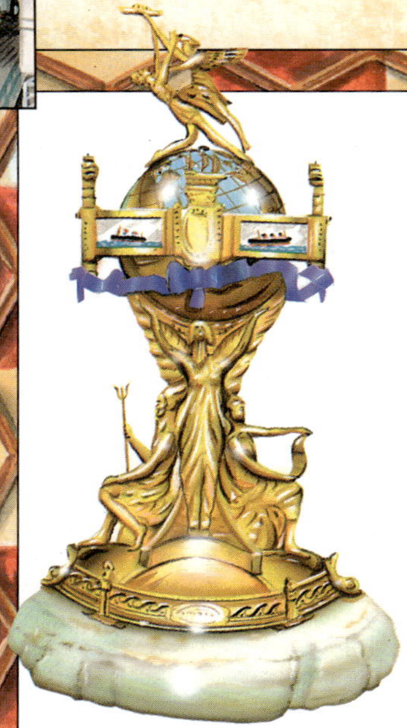

"BLUE RIBAND" AWARD

Before the high-speed craft of today, the fastest passenger ships afloat were giant liners competing for the "Blue Riband of the Atlantic," shown above. This trophy was awarded for the fastest Atlantic crossing.

WINNERS OF THE "BLUE RIBAND"

In June 1990 the world's biggest multi-hull, *Hoverspeed Great Britain*, crossed the Atlantic in three days, seven hours and 54 minutes. This broke the record of three days, ten hours and 40 minutes, which was set by the *United States* in 1952. The speed of the *Hoverspeed Great Britain* is compared, below, with the speeds of some of the previous winners.

1990 *Hoverspeed Great Britain* (36.65 knots)

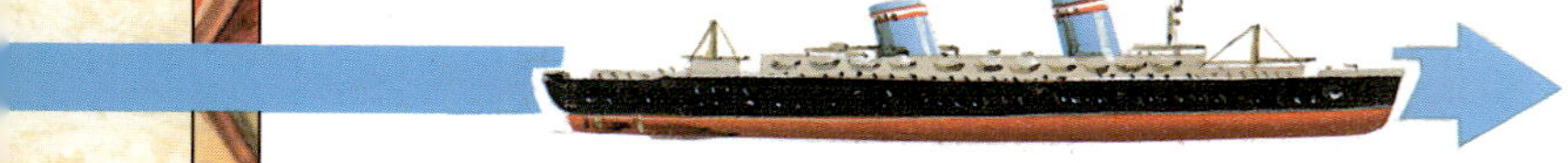

1952 *United States* (35.59 knots)

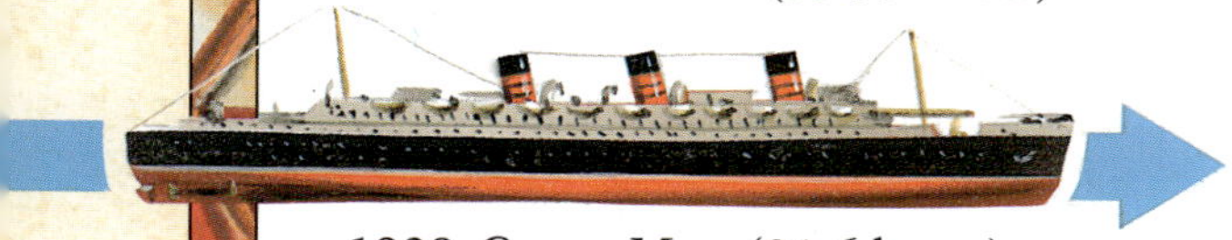

1938 *Queen Mary* (31.6 knots)

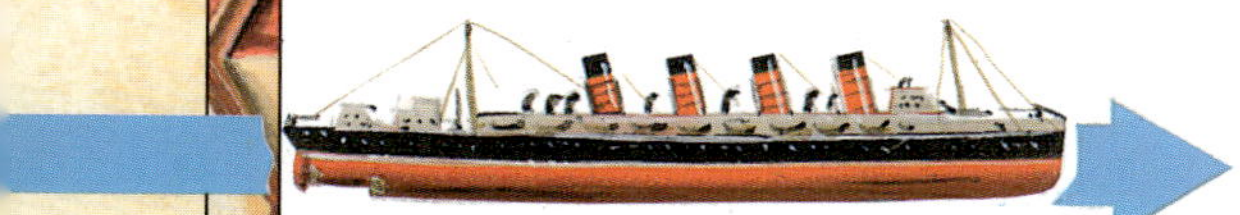

1907 *Mauretania* (27.4 knots)

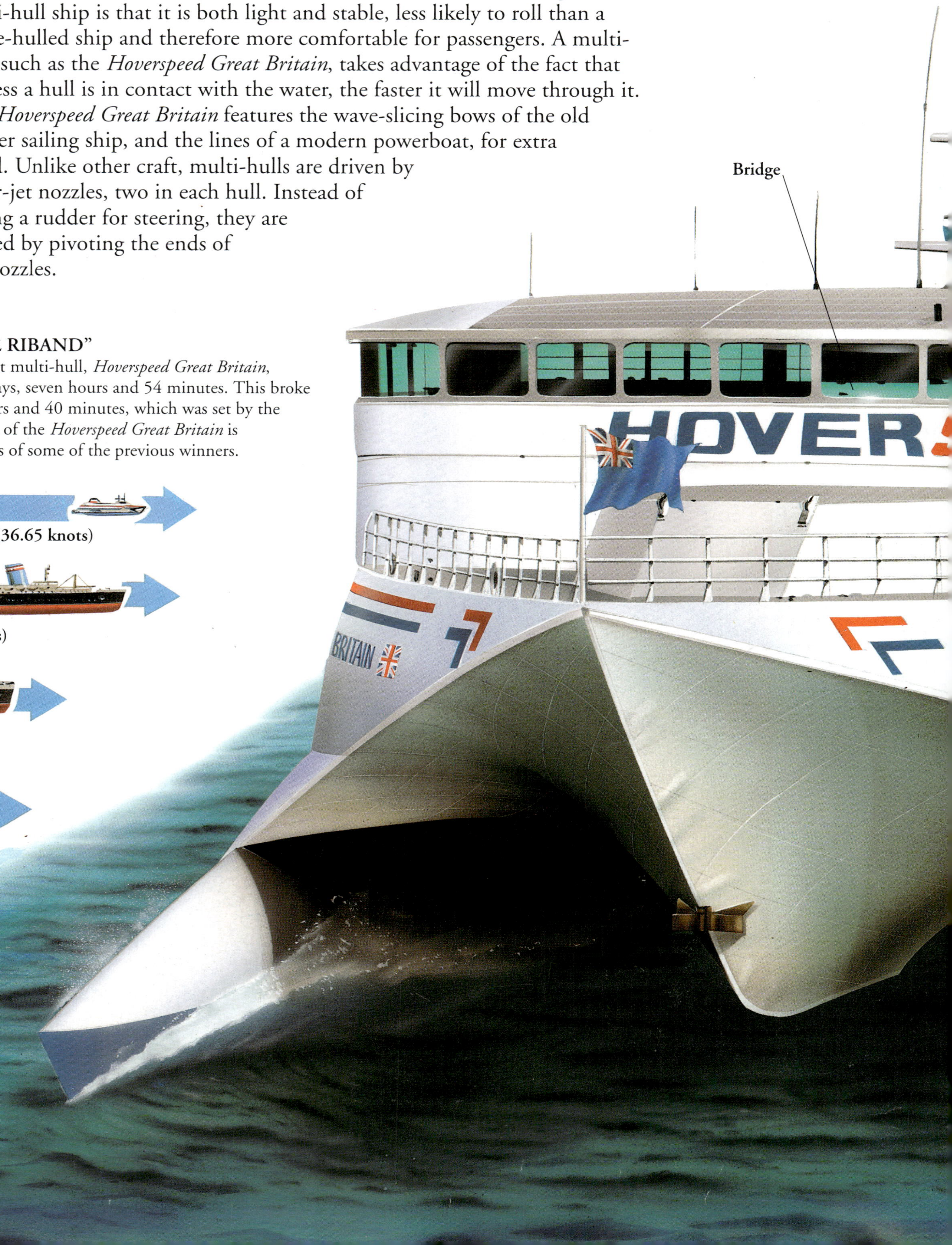

Bridge

"RO-RO" FERRIES

Some ferries have one or more vehicle decks stretching the length of the ship, with bow and stern doors. These are called "roll on, roll off" ferries. Large ones displace over 33,800 tons, carrying 1,600 passengers and 575 cars at 21 knots.

Passenger cabin
Features "airliner" seats and air conditioning

Observation gallery
Gives passengers a view of the sea on both sides

Bow
Wave-slicing bow designed to provide balance between high speed and passenger comfort

Jet-pipes
Nozzles direct the water jets to left and right.

Hull
Multi-hulled to prevent rolling

Engines
Four 16-cylinder Ruston diesel engines. Each produces 500 hp at 750 rpm.

The *Hoverspeed Great Britain* measures 243ft. (74m) long by 85ft. (26m) wide and displaces 3,050 tons. It can carry 432 passengers and 90 cars and has a service speed of 37 knots.

Radar scanner

Aft mast

Funnel

HOVERSPEED GREAT BRITAIN

Engine room vent inlets

"JET-PIPE" ENGINES

Fast multi-hulls are not driven by conventional shafts and screws. They use the same principle as an octopus or squid uses to swim: drawing in seawater and driving it out at great pressure through vent-pipes at the stern. Movable nozzles direct the jets to left and right, removing the need for a rudder.

What is a train?

A train is a vehicle with flanged wheels that is pulled by an engine along metal rails. An engine (or locomotive) supplies the power to pull the train behind it. The first trains were driven by steam power. Coal or wood was burned in a firebox to heat water in a boiler, which provided steam to drive pistons and then the wheels. Although the steam engine was invented in 1712, the first railroad locomotive was not built until 1804. Its engine had one horizontal cylinder and the driver had to walk next to it as it moved along at 5 miles (8 kilometers) per hour. By 1829, when a famous engine called the *Rocket* was built, the basic design included multitubed boilers and pistons that drove directly onto the driving wheels – the main wheels that move the train forward. For the next 125 years, almost all trains worked in the same way as the *Rocket*. Modern trains are usually powered by electricity: either directly, as in electric trains, or indirectly, as in diesel-electric trains.

CRESTS AND MAKERS' PLATES

Trains often display crests that show what line they belong to, or makers' plates that show who manufactured them.

HOW STEAM POWERS A LOCOMOTIVE

Fuel, such as coal or wood, is burned in the firebox. Heat from the fire passes along tubes in the boiler that are surrounded by water. The heat converts the water into steam, which collects at the top of the boiler and is passed along pipes to the cylinders. The pressure of the steam moves pistons in the cylinders. This movement is transmitted to the wheels by connecting rods. Exhaust steam and hot gases from the fire are forced through the blast pipe and out of the chimney.

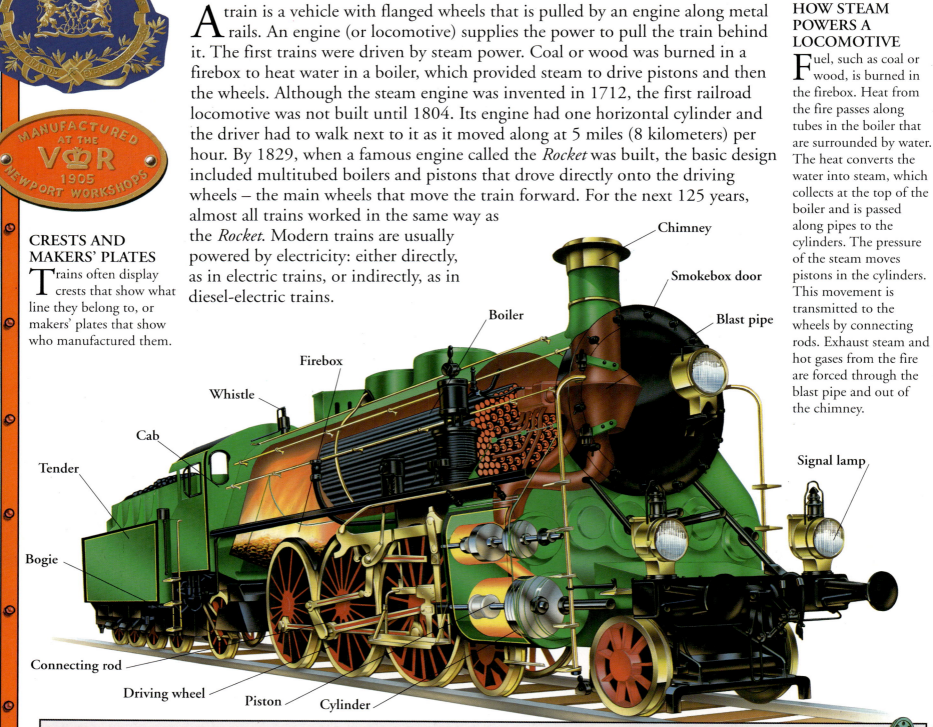

Chimney

Smokebox door

Blast pipe

Boiler

Firebox

Whistle

Cab

Tender

Signal lamp

Bogie

Connecting rod

Driving wheel

Piston

Cylinder

WHEEL ARRANGEMENTS

Steam trains had three kinds of wheels arranged in sets called bogies: carrying wheels in the front; driving wheels in the middle; and more carrying wheels at the back. Carrying wheels supported the engine, and the driving wheels were connected to the engine's power supply to make the train move.

4-4-0 or "American Eight-Wheeler" type. Four-wheeled leading bogie and four driving wheels.

4-6-2 or "Pacific" type. Four-wheeled leading bogie, six driving wheels and a two-wheeled trailing bogie.

4-8-4 or "Northern" type. Four-wheeled leading bogie, eight driving wheels and a four-wheeled trailing bogie.

STEAM DRIVING GEAR

Valve gears control the entry and exit of steam into and out of the cylinders on steam trains. The most widely used system of controlling the valves was invented in 1844 by the Belgian engineer Egide Walschaert, and is called Walschaert's valve gear. The movement of the valves and pistons inside the cylinders transmits driving action to the wheels through interconnecting rods.

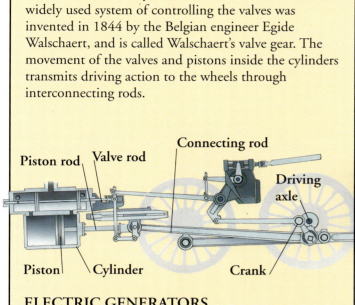

Piston rod   Valve rod   Connecting rod

Driving axle

Piston   Cylinder   Crank

ELECTRIC GENERATORS

Most modern diesel-electric locomotives are still based on a design introduced in the United States in 1924. On this "Deltic" diesel-electric locomotive, which was widely used by British Railways from 1960 to 1976, there are two 18-cylinder diesel engines that are used to power two direct-current electric generators.

Cooling fans

Engine

Main generator

PANTOGRAPHS

A pantograph on the roof of an electric locomotive collects power from overhead lines. It lies flat when not in use, which is about half the time: The pantograph can only pick up electricity going in one direction. There is one at each end of a car.

Overhead electric wires

THIRD RAIL COLLECTION

Some electric trains collect their power from a non-running third rail laid alongside the track. Electricity is collected by a metal collector shoe sliding along this rail.

Collector shoe

STEAM LOCOMOTIVES

Steam was the main form of power used to drive trains from the early 1800s, but it was not very efficient: Trains had to stop frequently to take on fuel and water. Coal was the fuel used to heat the water to make steam, except in North America, where wood was the main fuel used. Burning embers from the wood were caught in large smokestacks on American locomotives. Coal-burning steam trains can still be found today in developing countries.

DIESEL-ELECTRIC LOCOMOTIVES

Diesel-electric locomotives are used in areas where electric lines cannot be installed. They are, in effect, movable power stations and can travel long distances without refueling. A large tank of diesel fuel feeds a powerful diesel engine, which drives an electric generator. The generator provides the current through a transformer to power the traction motors, which turn the wheels.

ELECTRIC LOCOMOTIVES

An electric locomotive is the cleanest and most efficient form of railway motive power. High-voltage electricity is usually collected from overhead wires through a pantograph fitted on the roof. The electricity is passed through a transformer to the individual traction motors, mounted on bogies, which power the train. The continuous power supply means that electric trains can run for a long time at very high speeds.

47

Development of trains

Railroads have been in existence for over 250 years, from the time when carts on rails were pulled by horses. In 1804, the first steam locomotive, built by Richard Trevithick in England, pulled 10 tons and carried 70 passengers along a track. This new form of transportation caught on quickly. By 1820, engineers were inventing new designs to make the locomotives work better. By the 1830s, most locomotives followed a standard design based on steam power. This design was improved many times over the next 110 years. The first locomotive went only 5 miles (8 kilometers) per hour. In 1938, the world record for steam was set at 126 miles (202.7 kilometers) per hour. Soon, however, steam locomotives were replaced by diesel and electric engines, which were cleaner, more powerful and more economical. Electric railroads had begun operating as early as the 1890s, but the wires were too expensive to install over large areas such as the prairies of North America. Diesel-electric trains, which generated their own power, were developed for this reason. By the 1960s they had replaced steam in most of the world.

Locomotion
Steam, 1825
4 driving wheels
12mph (20kph)

LOCOMOTION

George and Robert Stephenson designed this engine specially to pull passenger carriages. It was first used on September 27, 1825, and was part of the first public railroad that carried passengers using a steam engine – the Stockton & Darlington Railway, England. The driver stood on a platform at the side of the engine. The coaches were very small.

LORD OF THE ISLES

To improve stability and make the journey more comfortable for passengers, the British engineer Daniel Gooch designed a broad-gauge 4-2-2 locomotive. The wide carriages traveled on a 7-foot 0.25-inch (214-centimeter) gauge track at speeds up to 70 miles (100 kilometers) per hour. The most famous broad-gauge locomotive was the *Lord of the Isles*.

Lord of the Isles
Steam, 1852
2 driving wheels
70mph (100kph)

TRAINS THROUGH THE AGES

The timeline shows some important events in the history of trains, and some of the trains that became famous.

1712: First steam engine built in England by Thomas Newcomen.

1804: First steam railroad locomotive built by Richard Trevithick of Cornwall, England.

1825: The first public railroad opens in England. The first North American steam locomotive is built by John Stevens.

1829: George and Robert Stephenson's *Rocket* wins the Rainhill Trials. It was one of the first locomotives on the Liverpool and Manchester Railway, the world's first intercity line.

1830: The South Carolina Railroad offers the first regular service in North America.

1831: The four-wheel bogie is invented in North America.

1863: First under-ground railroad operated by steam opens in London.

1869: The world's first transcontinental railroad is opened in the United States.

DOMINION OF NEW ZEALAND

Streamlined designs were introduced in the 1930s to improve aerodynamics, making trains look sleek and fast. However, the streamlined covers had to be removed for maintenance work. This Class A4 4-6-2 locomotive, *Dominion of New Zealand*, is identical to *Mallard*, which set the world speed record for steam in 1938 at 126 miles (202.7 kilometers) per hour.

> **Dominion of New Zealand**
> 1930s, steam
> 6 driving wheels
> 90mph (160kph)

TGV ATLANTIQUE

The current world rail speed record was set on May 18, 1990, by a specially modified French TGV Atlantique electric train. The TGV accelerated to 319 miles (515 kilometers) per hour on the new high-speed line from Le Mans to Tours. TGVs in daily service on new high-speed lines in France regularly reach speeds of up to 186 miles (300 kilometers) per hour.

> **TGV Atlantique**
> Electric, 1980s
> 8 driving wheels (each end)
> 319mph (515kph; world record set in 1990)

> **Maglev train**
> A.D. 2045?
> No wheels
> 496mph (800kph)

TRANSRAPID 06

Trains for the future are being designed without wheels, making them even faster. Prototypes of these "maglev" trains have been built already in Germany and Japan. Maglev trains use the principle of magnetic levitation, almost eliminating friction. Magnetic forces are able to propel the train at great speed. These high-speed trains will be ideal for long-distance travel, at speeds of up to 496 miles (800 kilometers) per hour.

1879: DC electric motor invented in Germany, making electric trains possible.

1881: First public electric railroad opens near Berlin, Germany.

1890: First electric underground train opens in London.

1938: *Mallard* sets the world steam speed record of 126 miles (202.7 kilometers) per hour.

1940s: Diesel locomotives begin to replace steam. They could travel longer distances in less time because they did not need to stop so often for refueling. The first diesel locomotive was built in Germany in 1913.

1941: Big Boy, the largest steam locomotive ever built, is produced in the United States for the Union Pacific Railroad.

1964: The first monorail line opens in Tokyo.

1994: The Channel Tunnel for trains between England and France opens.

1996: Maglev train opens at Disney World in Florida, running at 248 miles (400 kilometers) per hour.

Rocket

"It seemed to fly...it actually made me giddy to look at it."
An observer at the Rainhill Trials, 1829

PASSENGER COMFORT

First-class passenger coaches built for the Liverpool and Manchester Railway in 1830 were similar to stagecoaches. Although their design was simple compared with modern coaches, they had sprung buffers to absorb impact. The brakeman sat on the roof where passengers kept their luggage. Until 1844, third-class passengers traveled in coaches without a roof.

The *Rocket* was designed and built by George and Robert Stephenson. It was the first intercity steam locomotive, and it ran between Liverpool and Manchester. But it became well known for another reason. In 1829 a contest was held to find the best locomotive to run on George Stephenson's new Liverpool and Manchester Railway. *Rocket* was the only locomotive that was able to do everything that was required in the contest, and it was awarded the prize. It reached a speed of 29 miles (46.6 kilometers) per hour with a full load, and it was able to haul coachloads of passengers at 20 miles (32 kilometers) per hour up a steep slope. *Rocket*'s success was helped by some special technical features. These were a multitubed boiler that made steam quickly; tilting cylinders that powered the driving wheels using a connecting rod; a blast pipe that created a better draft for the fire by sending steam exhaust up the chimney; and a separate firebox covered by a water-jacket. Although many other steam trains were copied from *Rocket*'s basic design, *Rocket* itself was soon replaced on the railroad by an improved model called the *Planet* – also designed by the Stephensons – which gave a smoother ride.

Chimney

Steam dome

Boiler

Water tank

ROCKET

LIVERPOOL

Tender

Connecting rod

Driving wheel

50

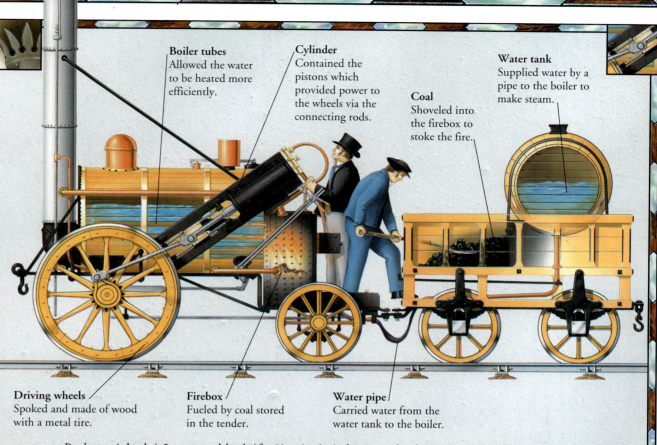

Boiler tubes
Allowed the water to be heated more efficiently.

Cylinder
Contained the pistons which provided power to the wheels via the connecting rods.

Coal
Shoveled into the firebox to stoke the fire.

Water tank
Supplied water by a pipe to the boiler to make steam.

Driving wheels
Spoked and made of wood with a metal tire.

Firebox
Fueled by coal stored in the tender.

Water pipe
Carried water from the water tank to the boiler.

Rocket weighed 4.5 tons and had 4ft. 8in. (1.4m) driving wheels. It ran on a 4ft. 8in. (143cm) gauge track. With its sprung wheels it reached speeds of up to 29mph (46.6kph). Later, when its cylinders were tilted less steeply, it was able to reach 50mph (80.45kph).

MAKING THE ROCKET MOVE

Rocket was powered by two outside cylinders. Steam passed from the boiler into the cylinders (1), where it pushed pistons down from the top (2), moving the wheel forward (3). When the piston had moved down the cylinder as far as it could, the valve slide moved to allow more steam in from the bottom (4). The steam pushed the piston back up the cylinder (5), pulling the wheel around.

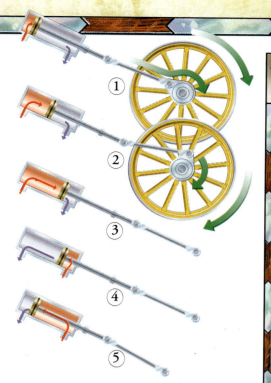

BUILDING THE LIVERPOOL AND MANCHESTER RAILWAY

Opposed by landowners, George Stephenson fought to obtain an Act of Parliament, allowing the railroad to be built. It was a huge civil engineering project. A bog had to be crossed, cuttings had to be blasted through rocks, and there were no machines – just teams of navvies using picks and shovels.

Irish Sea

Lancashire

LIVERPOOL — RAINHILL — MANCHESTER

Cheshire

THE RAINHILL TRIALS

A contest was held at Rainhill in October 1829 to find the best locomotive for the Liverpool and Manchester Railway. The locomotives had to haul 20 tons 15 times over 1.75 miles (2.8 kilometers) at 10 miles (16.09 kilometers) per hour. *Novelty* was fast but could not pull the load. *Sans Pareil* was too heavy and broke down. *Rocket* completed the task, and was awarded the prize.

THE LIVERPOOL AND MANCHESTER RAILWAY

This double-track railroad was engineered by George Stephenson. It was the world's first railroad to link two cities and run to a timetable. During its opening in 1830, William Huskisson, MP for Liverpool, was run over by *Rocket* ! Manchester's Liverpool Road Station is the world's oldest railroad station and is now part of a museum.

Rocket

Novelty

Sans Pareil

Lord of the Isles

THE GREAT WESTERN RAILWAY

The GWR was nick-named "God's Wonderful Railway." Its coat of arms combined those of London and Bristol. The GWR opened in 1840, engineered by Isambard Kingdom Brunel. He used a 7-foot 0.25-inch (214-centimeter) gauge track instead of the standard 4-foot 8.50-inch (143.5-centimeter) to give trains more stability. By 1848, trains traveled the 118 miles (190 kilometers) between London and Bristol in 2.5 hours, reaching 70 miles (96 kilometers) per hour.

The *Lord of the Isles* was a steam locomotive that ran on the Great Western Railway (GWR). This 4-2-2 engine was designed by Daniel Gooch, the railroad's locomotive superintendent. It was one of 29 Courier class locomotives and ran on the GWR's 7-foot 0.25-inch (214-centimeter) broad-gauge track. *Lord of the Isles* pulled express trains at speeds of 60 miles (96 kilometers) per hour between London, Birmingham and South West England. Built in 1851, it was displayed at the Great Exhibition, where it was known as *Charles Russell*. In 1852 it was renamed *Lord of the Isles* and was chosen to haul the railroad director's special train to celebrate the opening of the London–Birmingham line. Unluckily, it collided with another train on the way, but it survived this mishap to remain in service for many years. When it was withdrawn from use in 1884, it had traveled 790,000 miles (1,271,110 kilometers). Although it was broken up in 1906, its enormous 8-foot (2.4-meter)-diameter driving wheels were saved, and they can be seen today as a museum exhibit.

TWO GAUGES OF TRACK

Trains traveling on broad-gauge track could not use standard-gauge track. But in some places the wider broad gauge was laid alongside standard gauge to make what was called mixed-gauge track.

— **Standard gauge**
— **Mixed gauge**
— **Broad gauge**

Special wide carriage

Six-wheel tender

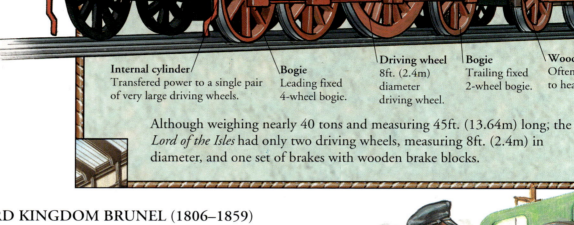

Smokebox
With blast pipe inside.

Boiler tubes
Multi-tubed boiler produced higher steam pressure.

Handbrake
With control handle.

Leaf springs
Provided basic suspension.

Internal cylinder
Transfered power to a single pair of very large driving wheels.

Bogie
Leading fixed 4-wheel bogie.

Driving wheel
8ft. (2.4m) diameter driving wheel.

Bogie
Trailing fixed 2-wheel bogie.

Wooden brake blocks
Often caught fire due to heat of friction.

Although weighing nearly 40 tons and measuring 45ft. (13.64m) long; the *Lord of the Isles* had only two driving wheels, measuring 8ft. (2.4m) in diameter, and one set of brakes with wooden brake blocks.

CHANGING GAUGES

The broad-gauge track of the GWR caused problems because it was wider than the standard railroad track used in the rest of Britain. The task of changing the GWR to the standard gauge began in 1869, after a Royal Commission ruled that the broad gauge must go. In May 1892, the conversion was finally finished using an army of over 4,000 men.

ISAMBARD KINGDOM BRUNEL (1806–1859)

Brunel was the engineer of the Great Western Railway from 1833 until his death, and designed the broad-gauge London–Bristol line. Although some of his early projects failed, his finest achievements include the Clifton Suspension Bridge and the steamships *Great Western* and *Great Britain*.

Chimney

Outer frame

Smokebox

THE CREW

The driver and fireman of the *Lord of the Isles* worked in an open-air cab. They needed to be hardy: The cab's small side-sheets and "spectacles," fitted on the backplate, gave them little shelter as they traveled at 60 miles (96 kilometers) per hour, sometimes through driving wind and rain. But on hot days there was no way to get away from the heat of the boiler.

53

The General

"The train toiled over this infinity like a snail; and being the one thing moving, it was wonderful what huge proportions it began to assume in our regard. It seemed miles in length, and either end of it within but a step of the horizon."

Robert Louis Stevenson, *Emigrant Train*

Promontory Point

0   1,000 miles

LINKING THE OCEANS

During the Civil War, Abraham Lincoln authorized the first railway across the United States. Two railroad companies, the Central Pacific from the West and the Union Pacific from the East, eventually linked up at Promontory Point in Utah on May 10, 1869.

The first North American steam-operated railroad opened in 1830 and by 1855 nearly 21,960 miles (35,420 kilometers) of track had been laid. Because of its ability to give a smoother ride on the roughly laid tracks, the 4-4-0 type of steam locomotive rapidly became the standard American locomotive used on nearly every railroad. The *General* was a typical wood-burning 4-4-0 locomotive of this period. Wood was used as fuel because this was more plentiful than coal in the Midwest. A large spark arrester was fitted to the chimney to help eliminate forest and grassland fires along the track. A massive cowcatcher was fitted at the front to provide protection on the unfenced lines. During the Civil War, from 1861 to1865, when large armies and supplies were moved by rail, the *General* became famous as a victim of kidnapping. Union soldiers captured the *General*, a Confederate locomotive, between Atlanta and Chattanooga. Hotly pursued for nearly 90 miles (145 kilometers) by another Confederate locomotive, *Texas*, the *General* eventually ran out of fuel. The kidnappers were hanged as spies.

Spark arrester

Bell

Chimney

FUELING THE *GENERAL*

Logs, cut from nearby forests, were loaded into the locomotive tender for fuel. Water for the boiler was fed by hose from water towers into large tanks, also contained in the tender. Sand, which enabled the locomotive to grip slippery rails, was stored in a huge dome on the top of the boiler.

Cowcatcher

Boiler
Turned water into steam.

Spark-arresting chimney
Reduced the risk of lineside fires.

Cab
Gave protection to driver and fireman.

Firebox
Logs were burned inside to heat the water.

Headlight
Oil-fueled lamp lit up the track at night.

Tender
Eight-wheeled double bogie.

The *General* was a wood-burning 4-4-0 locomotive of the American standard type with a characteristic chimney. The engine weighed 26.3 tons. It could develop over 350 horsepower and travel at speeds of up to 60mph (96kph) over roughly laid and uneven track.

Sand storage dome

TRACKLAYING IN THE MIDWEST

Early American railway track was built quickly and cheaply. Lightweight iron rail was spiked direct to wooden cross-sleepers, or "ties." A 10-mile (16-kilometer) stretch of the Central Pacific Railroad was laid in one day in 1869. This backbreaking work was mainly carried out by Chinese and Irish immigrant laborers.

AMBUSHED!

The rapid spread of railways into the American Midwest was relentless. Many of the lines were built through the territory of Native Americans, who tried to protect their land by attacking trains and destroying track. Outlaws and thieves also raided trains and robbed and terrorized passengers. Railroad workers and passengers soon had to carry guns to protect themselves.

Darjeeling–Himalayan Express

*"Up the hill goes the narrow-gauge train from Darjeeling to Ghoom,
and down the road comes Asia on foot."*
Peter Allen, *On the Old Lines*

The Darjeeling–Himalayan Railway climbs more than 6,000 feet (1,829 meters) up the steep slopes of the Himalayas. Opened in 1881, it was engineered by Franklin Prasage of the East Bengal Railway and was designed to follow the winding course of an old army road. It runs for 51 miles (82 kilometers) from the plains at Siliguri to the foothills of the Himalayas at Darjeeling. The main climb of 16 miles (25.75 kilometers) has a steep gradient averaging 1-in-29. To climb the slopes, switchbacks and loops are used instead of expensive tunnels and bridges. The first locomotives used on the line were eight small British 0-4-0 tank engines. Their short wheel base allowed them to ride along the tightly curving narrow-gauge track. By 1927, 32 locomotives of this type had been built. Some of them are still in use, and they can haul loads of up to 50 tons up a steep slope. The oldest surviving example now operates at the Railway Transport Museum, New Delhi, India.

THE ROUTE OF THE DARJEELING–HIMALAYAN RAILWAY

As it climbs from Siliguri (1) to Darjeeling (3), the railroad passes paddy fields, forests, tea plantations and mountain slopes. After 7 miles (11 kilometers), the route becomes steep and twisting. Trains stop to refuel at Kurseong (2) (4,799 feet; 1,463 meters). To climb higher, the trains have to reverse up four switchbacks and go around four loops. The journey ends 6,966 feet (2,133 meters) above sea level in Darjeeling.

Large headlight

Smokebox door

Coal bunker

Guard rail to protect sanding crew

GETTING A GRIP

In the monsoon season, 125 inches (300 centimeters) of rain can fall in a short time. Sand is sprinkled on steep track to help the locomotive's wheels grip the slippery rails. Most modern trains have built-in sanding equipment, but the Darjeeling–Himalayan engines also have a human sander who perches on the front of the locomotive dropping sand on the rails as the train moves slowly forward.

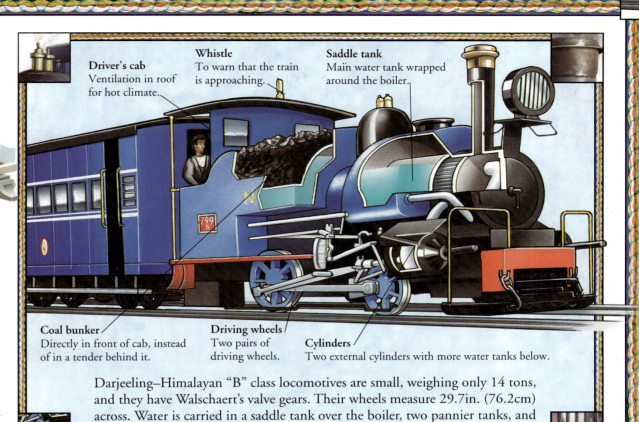

Driver's cab
Ventilation in roof for hot climate.

Whistle
To warn that the train is approaching.

Saddle tank
Main water tank wrapped around the boiler.

Coal bunker
Directly in front of cab, instead of in a tender behind it.

Driving wheels
Two pairs of driving wheels.

Cylinders
Two external cylinders with more water tanks below.

Darjeeling–Himalayan "B" class locomotives are small, weighing only 14 tons, and they have Walschaert's valve gears. Their wheels measure 29.7in. (76.2cm) across. Water is carried in a saddle tank over the boiler, two pannier tanks, and tanks under the cylinders.

GETTING A FREE RIDE

Rail travel is popular in India and trains can be very crowded. When there is no more room in the compartments – or to avoid paying the fare – some passengers cling to the roof or sides of the coach even though this is very dangerous. The roof is also used to stow baggage when the carriages become too crowded. The narrow-gauge Darjeeling–Himalayan train is so slow that passengers can leap off when the train is entering a loop and jump on again when it reaches the other side.

Narrow-gauge passenger coach

LOOPS AND SWITCHBACKS

Two ways in which railroads can scale heights are by using loops and switchbacks. In a loop (above), the line spirals until it crosses over itself. On the Darjeeling–Himalayan Railway, a loop at Batasia makes two spirals to take the train 140 feet (42.67 meters) higher. In a switchback (right), a train drives into a dead end and backs uphill into a second dead end before going forward up the mountain.

Orient-Express

VENICE SIMPLON ORIENT-EXPRESS
LONDON · PARIS · VENICE

"[For the first journey in 1883] Nagelmackers had spared no effort to ensure the success of this much-publicized trip, providing beautiful crystal and linen, elaborate food, exclusive wine and impeccable service."
Shirley Sherwood, *The Venice Simplon Orient-Express*

THE ORIENT-EXPRESS AS POPULAR CULTURE

This poster of the Orient Express is drawn in the Art Deco style in which the train was decorated in the 1930s. The Orient-Express has also starred in many books and movies. The most famous is Agatha Christie's *Murder on the Orient-Express*, filmed in 1974.

The famous Orient-Express made its first run from Paris to Constantinople (now Istanbul) in 1883. It was run by a Belgian company founded by Georges Nagelmackers. The train was the height of luxury and its lavish carriages were based on American Pullmans. Crossing seven countries, its journey of 1,853 miles (2,988 kilometers) took 67.5 hours. After the Simplon Tunnel was opened between Italy and Switzerland, the train was relaunched as the Simplon Orient-Express in 1919. Starting in Calais, France, it made journeys to Istanbul, Athens and Bucharest. By 1930, it had linked up with the Taurus Express, which went to Cairo in Egypt. By 1932, services also ran from Berlin, Ostend, Amsterdam, Vienna and Prague. The Simplon Orient-Express did not run during World War 2, and was withdrawn in 1977. But in 1982, with restored Pullman and Wagons-Lits carriages, it was launched as the Venice Simplon Orient-Express. The new service runs between London and Venice.

Official passenger list

Dining car

COMPAGNIE INTERNATIONALE DES WAGONS-LITS ET DES GRANDS EXPRESS EUROPEENS

Porter

Nº 3541

THE WAGONS-LITS COMPANY

Impressed by Pullman sleeping cars, the Belgian Georges Nagelmackers built the first European sleeping cars. He founded the Compagnie Internationale des Wagons-Lits (International Sleeping Car Company), which still exists today. This was the company that launched the Orient-Express in 1883. Its distinctive blue and gold logo adorned the original carriages and is used on the modern cars.

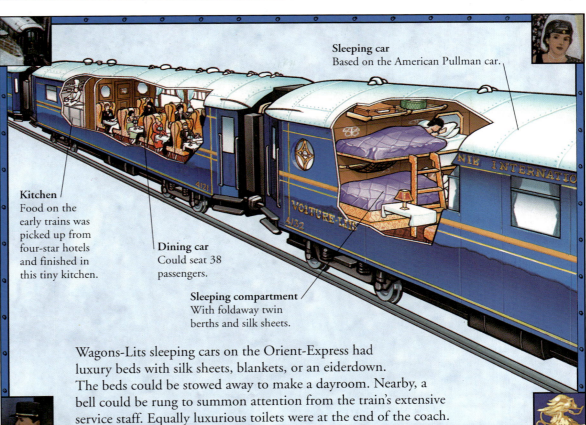

Sleeping car
Based on the American Pullman car.

Kitchen
Food on the early trains was picked up from four-star hotels and finished in this tiny kitchen.

Dining car
Could seat 38 passengers.

Sleeping compartment
With foldaway twin berths and silk sheets.

Wagons-Lits sleeping cars on the Orient-Express had luxury beds with silk sheets, blankets, or an eiderdown. The beds could be stowed away to make a dayroom. Nearby, a bell could be rung to summon attention from the train's extensive service staff. Equally luxurious toilets were at the end of the coach.

Locomotive

BOAT TRAIN

The Wagons-Lits sleeping compartments of the trains that crossed the English Channel – on the way from London to Paris – had to transfer to a boat. Carriage by carriage, the train was loaded onto large ferries to make the crossings.

LONDON TO CAIRO BY TRAIN

In 1930, the journey from London (1) to Cairo (5) by rail took seven days. Passengers crossed by ferry to Calais (2) to board the Simplon Orient-Express. It went as far as Istanbul (3), but passengers could take connecting lines as far as Baghdad (4) and Cairo. The train that went to Cairo was called the Taurus Express. Passengers had to get off the train and take a bus through much of Palestine, where there were no railroads.

DINING ON THE ORIENT-EXPRESS

Food for the meals originally came from four-star hotels in Paris, with fresh supplies picked up from stations during the journey. The size of the kitchen has grown with each new version of the train. Today's Venice Simplon Orient-Express has eight chefs and four dishwashers. Passengers have always dined in luxury, with rich menus and fine wines to choose from. The waiters on the original train wore powdered wigs, waistcoats and silk stockings. The dining cars of the 1930s were decorated with Art Deco designs by famous European artists.

Twentieth Century Ltd

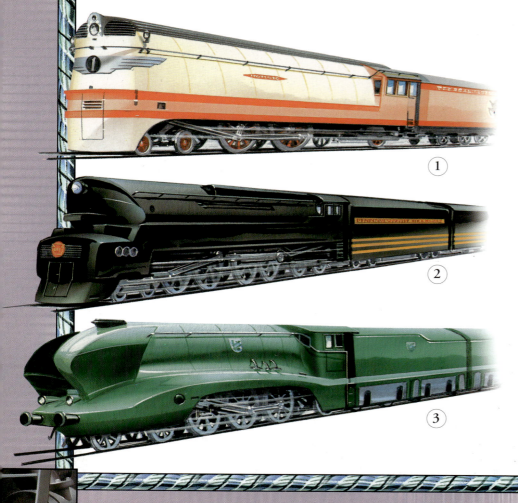

"At the zenith of steam operation in the United States, busiest among the great trunk routes were the rivals operating between New York and Chicago. The two world-famous trains were the Twentieth Century Limited and the Broadway Limited, with average speeds of 58mph {93kph}."

O. S. Nock, *World Atlas of Railways*

GRAND CENTRAL STATION, NEW YORK CITY

Passengers boarding the Twentieth Century Limited walked along a 259-foot-long (79-meter-long) maroon carpet laid out on the platform at Grand Central Station. This famous station has a cathedral-like concourse that is overlooked by the rococo-style Golden Clock, complete with a draped figure of Mercury and the American eagle. Under the clock was a favorite meeting place for people in New York. The station is now dwarfed by skyscrapers.

In 1902, the New York Central Railroad introduced the Twentieth Century Limited express to Chicago — then the second-largest city in the United States. By 1932 the train had become so popular that it had to be run in three separate sections, each with 13 cars. They left New York's Grand Central Station simultaneously at 2:45p.m. for the 20-hour journey. Electric haulage was used for the first 32 miles (51 kilometers) from New York to Harmon, where a Hudson 4-6-4 steam locomotive took over. Faster trains reduced the journey to 18 hours in 1932, and to 16 hours in 1938, when streamlined locomotives were introduced. The Twentieth Century Limited was very smart in appearance. It had a club and baggage car containing a bathroom, a barber's shop, a steward's pantry and a smoking lounge; nine sleeping cars; two dining cars; and an observation car. It had its own phone system and secretarial service. First-class passengers traveled in private luxury suites. Diesel locomotives were used after World War 2 until the service was stopped in 1967.

Streamlined nose covering smokebox

Handrail

Inspection cover

NEW YORK CENTRAL SYSTEM

STREAMLINING

In the 1930s many railroads introduced streamlined locomotives to reduce wind resistance and make the trains look sleek and fast. The 4-4-2 steam locomotive Hiawatha (1) was introduced in 1935 on the Milwaukee Railroad. The Pennsylvania Railroad introduced this Class T1 4-4-4-4 locomotive (2) in 1942. The Paris-Orleans railroad used 4-6-2 engines like this one (3) built in 1937.

THE ROUTE OF THE TWENTIETH CENTURY LIMITED

The 955 miles (1,541 kilometers) of the New York Central line followed the Hudson River and was mostly level. Engines and crews were changed at Syracuse and Toledo. Crews were changed also at Albany, Buffalo, Cleveland and Elkhart.

Driving wheels
Instead of spokes, the wheels had discs to reduce their weight and keep their rigidity and strength.

Boiler
Superheated steam passed twice through the boiler to make it extra hot.

Baker valve gear
A system of rods and bell cranks that replaced the Walschaert's valve gear on many modern American steam locomotives.

Cylinders
The 22in. (57cm) diameter cylinders had a 29in. (74cm) stroke.

The "Hudson" Class J-3a 4-6-4 locomotive that pulled the Twentieth Century Limited weighed 166 tons. Ten streamlined engines of this class were built by Alco for the New York Central in 1938. They were capable of hauling the 1,000-ton train at more than 100mph (160kph).

NEW YORK CENTRAL SYSTEM

NEW YORK CENTRAL

Streamlined stainless steel cars

Silver and blue livery

EXECUTIVE SERVICES

In the club and baggage car of the Twentieth Century Limited was a barber shop. The train's services also included a valet, the loan of an electric shaver or dictaphone, shoeshining, and complimentary newspapers.

Mallard

"There were no teething troubles with these engines – the finest possible tribute not only to Gresley's overriding direction, but to the detail design, to the workmanship and to the handling of the engine on the road."
O. S. Nock, *Sir Nigel Gresley*

Direction of travel

WORLD SPEED RECORD

On Stoke Bank in the United Kingdom on July 3, 1938, the LNER's locomotive *Mallard* reached 126 miles (202.7 kilometers) per hour) – the unbeaten record for a steam locomotive. A plaque with the record was mounted on the engine. *Mallard* is now on display in the National Railway Museum at York.

Mallard was a record-breaking steam locomotive run by the London and North Eastern Railway (LNER). It was one of 34 Class A4 4-6-2 locomotives used from 1935 to haul express trains between London and Edinburgh. They were designed by Sir Nigel Gresley, chief mechanical engineer of the LNER. Famed for their speed, these streamlined locomotives were based on the Great Northern 4-6-2s designed by Gresley, and they became his best-known achievement. One named *Silver Link* reached a record speed of 112 miles (181 kilometers) per hour just before the famous *Silver Jubilee* express was launched in September 1935. In 1937, the London, Midland and Scottish Railway set a new record of 113 miles (183 kilometers) per hour using a Coronation class 4-6-2. This spurred the LNER to try to regain the speed record. In July 1938, *Mallard* was fitted with a double chimney and coupled to a special test train that had a dynamometer car to monitor its speed. As *Mallard* sped south from Grantham, the driver gave it maximum steam all the way to Stoke summit. Then, as *Mallard* raced downhill, its speed rose to a world steam record of 126 miles (202.7 kilometers) per hour.

COLLECTING WATER AT HIGH SPEED

Because long-distance steam engines used a lot of water, water troughs were placed on main lines. Invented by John Ramsbottom, they were first used in 1860 by the London and North West Railway in North Wales. As each train sped over the troughs, an automatic scoop fitted under its tender was lowered to collect hundreds of gallons of water in a few seconds.

THE DRIVER

With his hand on the regulator, the driver is watching out for the next signal along the line. Drivers of locomotives like *Mallard* were responsible for the safety of hundreds of passengers. Unlike the drivers of modern trains, they had to do most tasks manually. They did not have fail-safe braking systems, or computer-controlled signals that could stop the train if the driver did not respond correctly in time.

THE CORONATION STREAMLINER

The Coronation was a 4-6-2 train that ran at high speeds between London and Edinburgh on the London, Midland and Scottish line from 1937. It had two-tone blue coaches hauled by locomotives with matching livery. Its open-plan design enabled passengers to be served with meals. In the summer months, for a small extra fee, first-class passengers could sit in a beaver-tail viewing car with large windows and armchairs to view the scenery.

CORONATION   1719

LNER

THE PROBLEMS WITH STREAMLINING

In the 1930s, many railroads around the world fitted panels to their express trains to make them streamlined. The panels looked sleek but had to be removed when the train was cleaned or repaired. The fireman of *Mallard* had to move two panels before he could clear out the cinders in the smokebox.

Whistle
All engines in this class had American chime whistles.

Double chimney
Enabled exhaust steam and smoke to exit more efficiently.

Boiler
Had a record output of 40,000lb. (18,144kg) of steam per hour.

Streamlined panels
Deflected smoke and soot away from the driver's cab.

Smokebox door
Hidden by streamlined cover.

External cylinders
Measured 16in. (41.9cm) by 28in. (71.1cm).

Driving wheels
Partially covered by streamlined panels.

Mallard weighed 165 tons and was 70ft. (21.6m) long. It had three cylinders and six driving wheels, which were 6ft. 8in. (2.03m) in diameter. Its eight-wheel corridor tender carried 5,000 gallons (18,925 liters) of water as well as eight tons of coal. The internal mechanical design was also streamlined.

Handrail

Nameplate

Streamlined nose

Signal lamp

MALLARD

N⁰ 4468

Buffer

Gun train

"We will flatten them [the Russians] like a hailstorm."
Adolf Hitler, ordering an
attack on Russia in 1941

Schwere Gustav (or "Heavy Gustav") was the name given to the biggest gun ever built. Before World War 2 (1939–1945), Adolf Hitler decided to have the gun made to smash the huge concrete defenses on the French Maginot Line. *Gustav* was designed to run on specially made double tracks. Its size made it difficult to manufacture, and by the time it was finished by the German firm Krupp in 1941, it was too late for it to be used against France.

Of the two guns finally made, only *Gustav* was used; In 1942 it was fired during the German siege of Sevastopol, a fortified Russian port. Four long trains were needed to transport the parts of the gun from Germany to the siege. It took 1,500 men a month to assemble it. Then 500 men were needed to operate it and to protect it with antiaircraft weapons and spotter planes. Its giant shells could be fired only once every 15 minutes, but they could hit targets almost 30 miles (48 kilometers) away. Although only 48 shells were fired, they destroyed Sevastopol's concrete defenses. (The people of Sevastopol had plenty of time to take cover underground while *Gustav* was put together!) After the Germans captured Sevastopol, *Gustav* was taken apart. Rather than let the weapon fall into Allied hands at the end of the war, the Germans bombed its carrying cars to destroy it.

Barrel

GUSTAV'S SHELLS

Two types of shell were fired from *Gustav's* 31.5-inch (81-centimeter) barrel: A shell weighing 10,526 pounds (4,763 kilograms), and a 15-foot (4.63-meter) shell weighing over 15,500 pounds (7,030 kilograms), which could pierce concrete. The charges (on the right) were kept separately.

A JEEP ON RAILS

When the U.S. army was advancing through Europe in 1944, some of their Willys jeeps were fitted with flanged wheels so they could travel on railroad lines. This meant they could bypass roads that were damaged or clogged with traffic.

Double tracks

TROOP AND ARMORED TRAINS OF WORLD WAR 1

During World War 1 (1914–1918), railroads were used to carry troops and supplies to battle fronts. Many railroad bridges, stations and tunnels were attacked and destroyed. German troop trains (1) transported soldiers long distances to the Russian front. The French troop train (2) had wagons, each carrying 40 soldiers, and flat trucks bearing guns and horse-drawn vehicles. The first British armored trains (3) had guns taken from old ships and were used to defend the coastline.

TRAVERSING THE GUN

Gustav ran on a sheltered double track, 0.75 miles (1.2 kilometers) long. The track was curved so that the barrel could be moved to different angles (traversed) to fire in different directions. The barrel itself could not move very much, so the whole gun was moved back and forth along the track according to where the target was.

Electric hoists
Shells and charges were hauled up to the loading deck one at a time.

Hydraulic rammer
For ramming the projectile and charge accurately.

Loading deck
A round took at least 15 minutes to load.

Barrel
28.9m long, firing shells more than 4m long.

Cradle
Specially built to support the enormous weight.

Generator
Provided power for ammunition hoists and for all lights and electric equipment.

Diesel engine
Each engine provided 1,000hp.

Control room
Where a German colonel commanded the full crew of 500.

Gustav was a massive weapon. Its total weight was 1,329 tons (1,349,970kg). Its barrel was 95ft. (29m) long and had a bore of 31.5in. (81cm). The barrel could tilt upward to 65 degrees, and could fire a giant shell a distance of nearly 30mi. (48km).

Recoil cylinder

Shell loading deck

Crane

DESTROYING ENEMY RAIL LINES

Because of their importance during World War 2, the railroads of Germany and occupied France were bombed by Allied air forces. The main targets were locomotive yards, sheds and works, plus junctions, stations, bridges and tunnels. Damaging the railroad network helped to slow down the movement of goods and supplies to the German army.

Big Boy

" The type got its name when someone at Alco chalked 'Big Boy' on the smokebox of one under construction."
George H. Drury, *Guide to North American Steam Locomotives*

Big Boy was the nickname given to the biggest and strongest steam locomotives ever made. The 25 articulated 4-8-8-4 steam locomotives were built between 1941 and 1944 by the Union Pacific Railroad at the Schenectady Works belonging to Alco. Big Boys were huge: They weighed 534 tons and were 16 feet (4.88 meters) high and 132 feet 9 inches (40.5 meters) long. The earliest locomotive would have fitted twice into Big Boy's tender, and Big Boy's coal-burning grate alone was almost 17 square yards (14 square meters). These giant locomotives were designed to haul 70-car freight trains, weighing 3,000 tons, over the Rocky Mountains. During World War 2 they were used as troop trains, hauling in pairs to transport heavy goods and soldiers across the country to the West Coast. Building up 7,000 horsepower, they would speed along at up to 70 miles (129 kilometers) per hour, eating up 10 tons of coal and more than 650 gallons (2,500 liters) of water in an hour. They were replaced by diesel locomotives in 1962, but several of them can still be seen in railroad museums.

Warning bell

Leading bogies

Headlight

Handrail

Cowcatcher

Rocket 0-2-2 (1829) UK:
Length 21ft. 6in.: cylinder diameter 8in.
Tractive effort 900lb.

Lord of the Isles 4-2-2 (1851) UK:
Length 45ft.: cylinder diameter 18in.
Tractive effort 7,000lb.

Mallard 4-6-2 (1935) UK:
Length 71ft.: cylinder diameter 18.5in.
Tractive effort 35,455lb.

Challenger 4-6-6-4 (1936) USA:
Length 125ft.: cylinder diameter 23in.
Tractive effort 57,238lb.

Big Boy 4-8-8-4 (1941) USA:
Length 132ft. 9in.: cylinder diameter 23in.
Tractive effort 74,323lb.

PULLING POWER

From *Rocket* to Big Boy, steam locomotives became bigger and more powerful with every model. It is difficult to compare this power because an engine's performance varies with weather and other conditions. A train that can pull a 3,000-ton load on a level track may only be able to pull 2,000 tons up a hill. For this reason, power is usually measured as tractive effort – the force exerted by a locomotive at the driving wheels.

THE UNION PACIFIC RAILROAD

In 1869, the first trans-American railroad was formed when the Union Pacific Railroad linked with the Central Pacific at Promontory Point in Utah. By 1900 the Union Pacific's main lines went from Ogden, Utah, to Council Bluffs, Iowa, and from Denver, Colorado, to Kansas City, Missouri. Huge locomotives hauled heavy freight trains over the mountains.

GOING AROUND THE BEND

Long steam locomotives had to be articulated so they could go around curves. Including its tender, Big Boy had 38 wheels arranged in six sections. Four of these were pivoted. The two sets of driving wheels were driven by separate sets of cylinders powered by a large boiler.

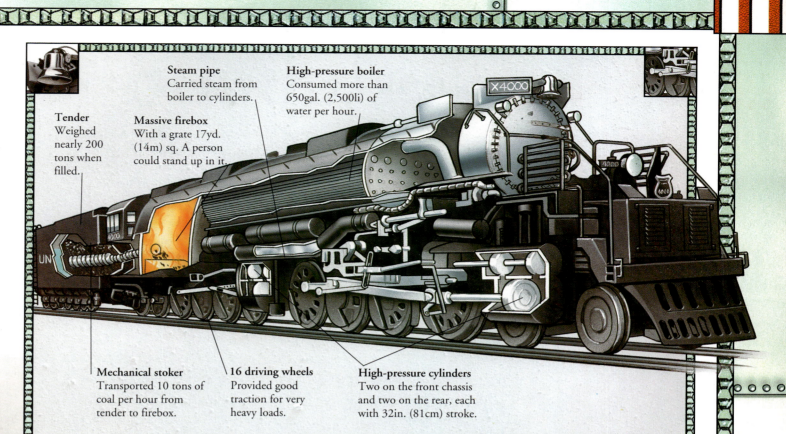

Tender
Weighed nearly 200 tons when filled.

Steam pipe
Carried steam from boiler to cylinders.

Massive firebox
With a grate 17yd. (14m) sq. A person could stand up in it.

High-pressure boiler
Consumed more than 650gal. (2,500li) of water per hour.

Mechanical stoker
Transported 10 tons of coal per hour from tender to firebox.

16 driving wheels
Provided good traction for very heavy loads.

High-pressure cylinders
Two on the front chassis and two on the rear, each with 32in. (81cm) stroke.

Everything about Big Boy was oversized. With its tender, it weighed 534 tons and was 132ft. 9 in. (40.5m) long. With a tractive effort of up to 61 tons, it was able to haul trains weighing more than 3,000 tons at 70mph (129kph). Four high-pressure cylinders powered 16 driving wheels. The 14-wheel tender held 20,668 gallons (79,493 liters) of water and 28 tons of coal. The coal was fed into the massive firebox by a mechanical stoker.

TURNING AROUND

At the end of each journey, steam locomotives with tenders had to be turned 180 degrees. This was done on a turntable in the middle of a special round building. The turntable consisted of a piece of track on a pivot in a circular pit. It was powered by electricity or by steam from a locomotive. The world's longest turntable (135 feet; 41 meters) was built in the United States for Big Boy.

Two sets of eight driving wheels

Trailing bogie

Settebello

"The Settebello is named for an Italian card game, the Lucky Seven. The driving controls are located in an upper flight deck, above the lounge, exactly in the style of the first class section in the jumbo jet airliner – but the arrangement was used in the Settebello first."
O. S. Nock, *World Atlas of Railways*

Settebello was a high-speed luxury train that ran between Rome and Milan on the Italian State Railways. It was introduced in 1953 as transportation for business executives in a hurry, and for wealthy tourists who could afford the high price of the tickets – almost double the ordinary first-class fare. Airlines were not yet offering internal shuttle flights, and the Settebello was much faster and more comfortable than any car. At its top running speed of 110 miles (180 kilometers) per hour, it was like a very fast five-star hotel on wheels. Up to 190 passengers sat in 15 spacious first-class lounges with full-size armchairs and sofas. The lounges were very quiet and restful, because the coaches had been completely soundproofed. There were showers on board, and the whole train was air-conditioned. The interior was elegantly decorated, and the exterior was painted in silver-gray and green.

The 391-mile (630-kilometer) journey from Milan to Rome took five and a half hours. Settebello shared the high-speed *Direttissima* (most direct) line with another express train to Rome that left only seven minutes later, but Settebello stayed well ahead. The line traveled through the Appennine Mountains and ran through 18 miles (29 kilometers) of tunnels, including the 11.5-mile (18.5-kilometer) Galleria del Appenino, the world's second-longest main line tunnel. Settebello remained in service until the 1970s.

Adjustable window blinds

SETTEBELLO AND THE DIRETTISSIMA

Settebello provided a luxury high-speed service between Milan and Rome. It traveled on the *Direttissima* line, which opened in 1934 and passes directly through the Appennine Mountains. The train stopped at Bologna and Florence on the way.

LUCKY SEVEN

Settebello got its name from an Italian card game, Il Settebello, or "The Lucky Seven." This was because Settebello had seven cars: two power units in front, three cars in the middle, and another two units at the back. This meant that the train did not need separate locomotives at each end, and it would not have to change direction at the terminus in Florence.

FIRST-CLASS TRAVEL

Settebello was a luxury train. Only first-class passengers used its services. All seats were reserved and passengers were seated by a conductor. The train's center car had a spotless electric kitchen and an office for the two attendants. Next door was an elegant restaurant. Italian meals were provided by the Wagons-Lits Company, which ran the world-famous Orient-Express.

68

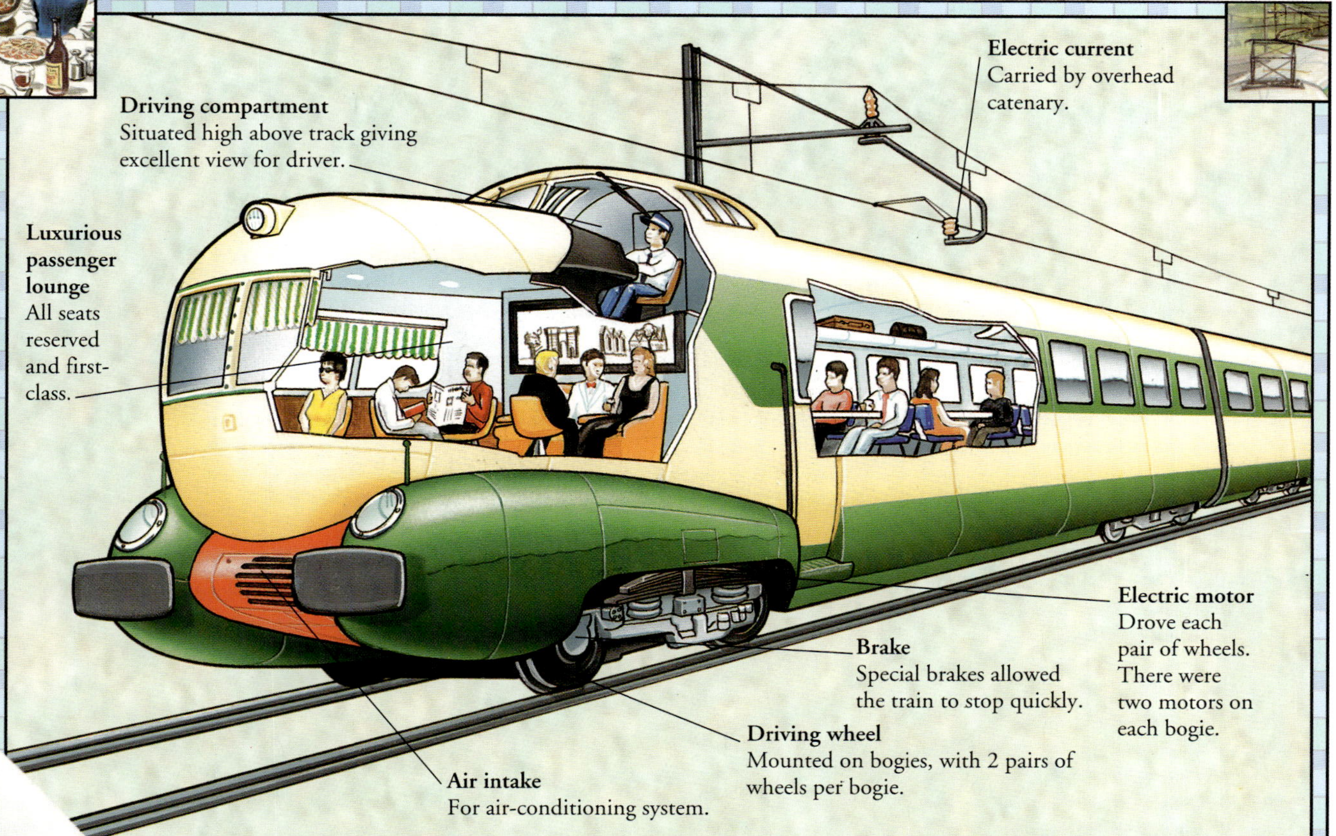

Driving compartment
Situated high above track giving excellent view for driver.

Electric current
Carried by overhead catenary.

Luxurious passenger lounge
All seats reserved and first-class.

Electric motor
Drove each pair of wheels. There were two motors on each bogie.

Brake
Special brakes allowed the train to stop quickly.

Driving wheel
Mounted on bogies, with 2 pairs of wheels per bogie.

Air intake
For air-conditioning system.

With its seven articulated cars, Settebello was 541ft. (165m) long, weighed 327 tons and reached 112mph (180kph). It was a Type ETR 300 electric multiple-unit train made at the famous Breda works. Using 3,000 volts DC, its motors generated 2,415hp.

RAILROAD TERMINUS

Settebello served the two great Italian cities of Rome and Milan. The railroad terminus at Rome (shown on the right) was built in the 1960s. Its modern design, using steel and glass, made the inside seem spacious and full of light – more like a new airport than an old-fashioned train station. The station matched the modern appearance of its most famous train.

Headlight

Buffer

THE VIEW FROM THE CAB

The driver's cab on Settebello was set 12 feet (3.66) meters above the track, above and behind the observation lounge. It gave the driver a full view of the line ahead. With a control panel in front of two seats, the cab was like a jet cockpit. The driver could maintain high speeds on the specially constructed line.

West Coast Postal

*"This is the night mail crossing the border,
Bringing the cheque and the postal order,
Pulling up Beattock, a steady climb –
The gradient's against her but she's on time."*
W. H. Auden, "Night Mail"

The West Coast Postal is one of the busiest British Traveling Post Office trains. It has run nightly from London to Scotland for over 100 years. It has no passengers, but post office staff travel on the train to sort mail for hundreds of destinations.

In the 1950s, the train, as shown here, consisting of up to 14 specially built mail and sorting coaches, left London Euston Station, usually hauled by a powerful Coronation class locomotive, at 8:30 p.m., arriving at Aberdeen at 8:15 the next morning. On its long journey north the West Coast Postal would stop to put down and pick up mail at main railway stations on the West Coast main line. A feature of this train was the mailbag transfer coach where mail could be picked up and set down automatically while the train was traveling at speed. The West Coast Postal train still runs, but its mail-exchange apparatus was last used for exchanging mail bags in 1971.

SUSPENDING THE MAIL

Heavy leather pouches, each containing 30 pounds (13.6 kilograms) of mail from the local sorting office for collection, were suspended at night from special trackside apparatus by post office staff at more than 20 strategic points along the route.

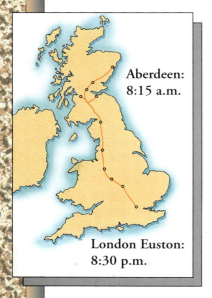

Aberdeen: 8:15 a.m.

London Euston: 8:30 p.m.

ROUTE OF THE WEST COAST POSTAL

The West Coast Postal departs every night from London Euston, stopping to transfer mail at Rugby, Tamworth, Crewe, Preston, Carlisle, Stirling and Perth, before arriving in Aberdeen the next morning. Parts of the train also go to Glasgow and Edinburgh.

PICKING UP THE MAIL

As the train traveled through the night at speeds of up to 62 miles (100 kilometer) per hour, a net was lowered from the side of the mailbag transfer coach. An alarm bell rang to warn the post office staff as the net scooped the suspended leather pouches from the trackside apparatus and they arrived with a loud bang in the sorting coach. The mail in the pouches was then sorted for delivery at stations farther down the line.

Cylinder

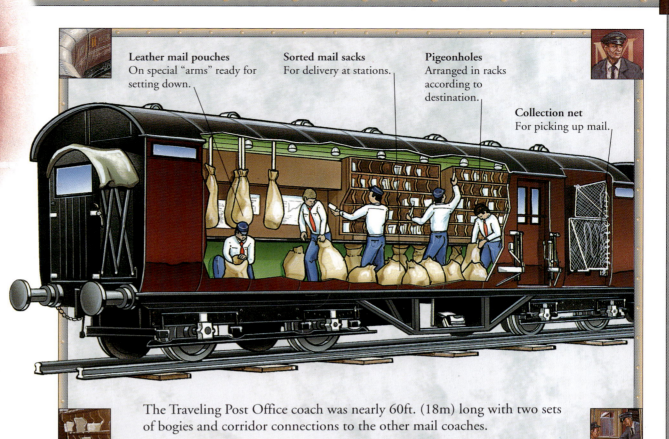

Leather mail pouches
On special "arms" ready for setting down.

Sorted mail sacks
For delivery at stations.

Pigeonholes
Arranged in racks according to destination.

Collection net
For picking up mail.

The Traveling Post Office coach was nearly 60ft. (18m) long with two sets of bogies and corridor connections to the other mail coaches.

MAILBOXES IN MAIL COACHES

At stations, the public could drop a letter directly into a mailbox situated in the side of a Traveling Post Office coach. An extra stamp had to be fixed to the letter to cover the cost of late collection.

Chimney

Smokebox

Smoke deflector

46256

1/8

SORTING THE MAIL

Each Traveling Post Office sorting coach was a hive of activity. Ten post office workers quickly sorted mail into a large rack of destination pigeonholes. Sorted mail was then placed in mail sacks, each with the name of its own district, hanging behind them ready for delivery at the next station, or put into leather pouches for setting down mail while on the move.

TRANSFERRING MAIL AT STATIONS

Mailbags from local sorting offices were delivered to the Traveling Post Office train at stations along the line. As the train was scheduled to stop for only a few minutes, staff had to work fast to load the bags into the coaches. At the same time, sorted mail from the train was taken off and loaded onto post office vans. Mail for other destinations was also transferred between trains at certain stations.

Buffer

Puffing Billy

"Only the efforts of a small but determined band of local citizens stand between Puffing Billy and an ignominious retirement."
The Age (Victoria, Australia), March 26, 1954

The much-loved Puffing Billy Railway in Australia is an 8-mile (13-kilometer) section of a 30-inch (76.2-centimeter) narrow-gauge line built outside Melbourne in 1900 by Victorian Railways. Set in the scenic Dandenong Mountains, it ran a rural route from Upper Fern Tree Gully to Gemsbrook, passing through Belgrave and Lakeside. Its purpose was to serve the growing village settlements, taking their fruit crops to Melbourne, and timber from nearby forests. Fitted with "cowcatchers," the two tank locomotives first used on the line were built by Baldwin Locomotives Works in Philadelphia (U.S.A.). Tourists enjoyed the railroad, but it was closed in 1953 after part of it was destroyed by a landslide. In 1958, the section from Upper Fern Tree Gully to Belgrave was rebuilt as a broad-gauge electric railroad linking with Melbourne. In 1954, the Puffing Billy Preservation Society was formed to try to reopen the narrow-gauge railroad from Belgrave to Lakeside. The first section was opened in 1964. The Puffing Billy Railway uses original locomotives that have been restored. The trains are made up of observation cars and open-sided carriages. Volunteers are now restoring another 6 miles (10 kilometers) of track.

STEAM GAUGE

The steam pressure gauge used on Puffing Billy is one of the original instruments, restored and in full working order. The engineer keeps an eye on it as he feeds coal to the firebox and water to the boiler.

AUSTRALIA'S FIRST PRESERVED RAILWAY

Although the Puffing Billy Railway has been owned by the Emerald Tourist Railway Board since 1977, its survival is due partly to the hard work of volunteers, who have been active since 1954. Helped by the army, they have rebuilt stations and relaid the track broken by the landslide, and have restored old steam engines to full working order.

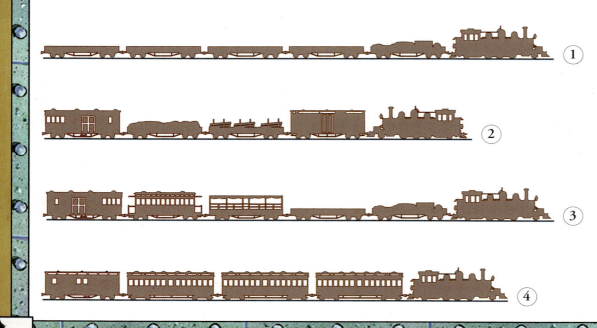

FREIGHT AND PASSENGERS

Several varieties of trains ran on the Puffing Billy Railway: long, open wagons carrying timber cut in the forest (1); goods trains with farm produce such as dairy foods and fruit being taken to markets in Melbourne (2); combined passenger and goods trains, usually with the passenger cars to the rear (combining the trains reduced the cost of running them) (3); tourist trains with open-sided carriages. These were popular for excursions from the city and could carry several hundred passengers in up to eight carriages (4).

MANUFACTURED AT THE VR 1905 NEWPORT WORKSHOPS

AUSTRALIA'S STEAM HERITAGE

Puffing Billy locomotives are 2-6-2 tanks. The first two of these were supplied by the American Baldwin company. After the railroad had been opened, more 2-6-2 tank locomotives were made at the Victorian Railways' workshops in Newport, Australia, and fitted with Westinghouse vacuum brakes. Special wagons were built to carry the locomotives on the broad-gauge network to the narrow-gauge Puffing Billy line.

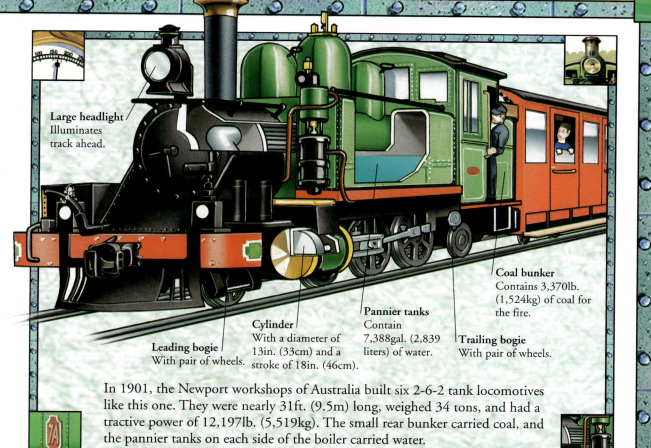

Large headlight Illuminates track ahead.

Leading bogie With pair of wheels.

Cylinder With a diameter of 13in. (33cm) and a stroke of 18in. (46cm).

Pannier tanks Contain 7,388gal. (2,839 liters) of water.

Trailing bogie With pair of wheels.

Coal bunker Contains 3,370lb. (1,524kg) of coal for the fire.

In 1901, the Newport workshops of Australia built six 2-6-2 tank locomotives like this one. They were nearly 31ft. (9.5m) long, weighed 34 tons, and had a tractive power of 12,197lb. (5,519kg). The small rear bunker carried coal, and the pannier tanks on each side of the boiler carried water.

THE END OF THE LINE

The first section of restored track between Belgrave and Lakeside already offers passengers an historic 8-mile (13-kilometer) journey. The remaining 6 miles (10 kilometers) of track from Lakeside through Cockatoo (1) to Gemsbrook (2) is currently being restored.

BUSHFIRE HAZARDS

In February 1926, many bushfires sprang up along the route of the Puffing Billy Railway. Several times as the train rattled its way through the burning hills, passengers stared in terror through the carriage windows at the huge flames trying to swallow up the track.

The Canadian

"The track along the northern shores of Lake Superior was a terrible section to build, cutting a ledge in towering walls of rock rising sheer from the waters of the lake."
O. S. Nock, *World Atlas of Railways*

In 1953, the Canadian Pacific Railway ordered 173 stainless steel cars from the American Budd company to make a new trans-Canadian train called the Canadian. It was launched in 1955 to run daily services between Montreal and Vancouver, and is still in service, mostly for tourists. For most of the journey, the Canadian is hauled by two diesel-electric locomotives of 1,500 horsepower, one with a driver's cab. A third locomotive is added to help the train cross the mountains. The cars are lightweight stainless steel for speed, and painted to match the engine. The train looks very striking as it threads its way through the Canadian Rockies. Seven complete sets of cars are required to run the service. Each train has dining cars, sleeping cars, 60-seat luxury coaches, an observation car, a dome-roofed buffet car with a kitchen, and a car with living quarters for the train's staff.

DRIVING THE CANADIAN

On long-distance North American trains, drivers use a telephone to speak to staff elsewhere on the train, and a radio-telephone link to speak to train controllers. During the Canadian's three-day journey, the crew is changed several times.

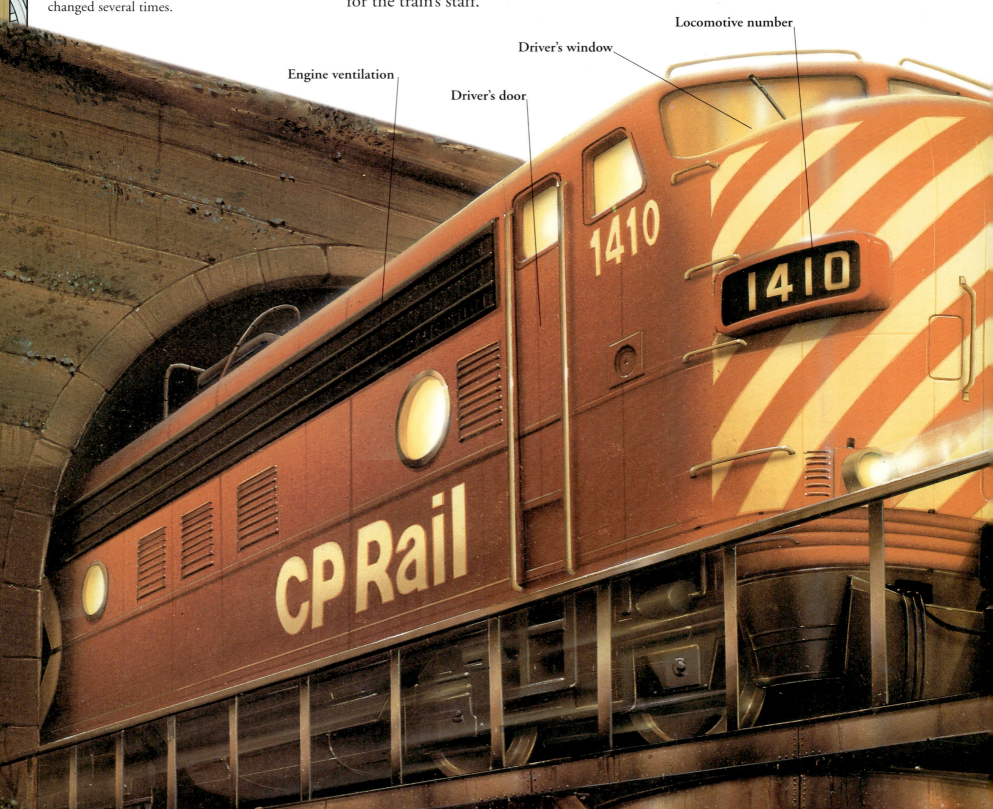

Engine ventilation

Driver's door

Driver's window

Locomotive number

1410

1410

CP Rail

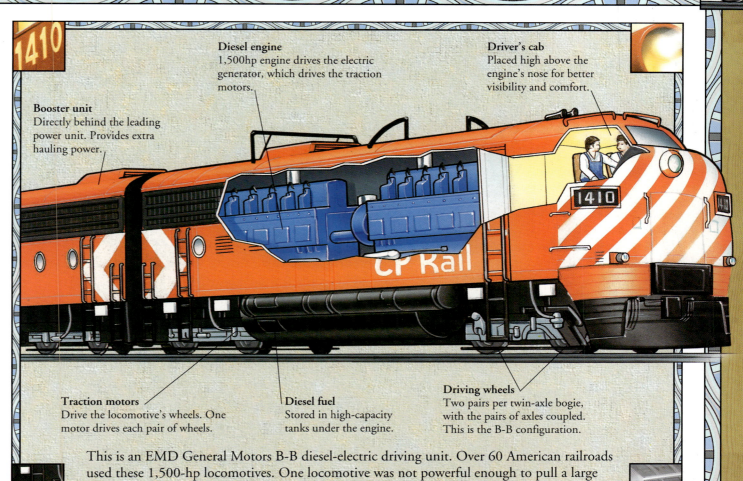

1410

Booster unit
Directly behind the leading power unit. Provides extra hauling power.

Diesel engine
1,500hp engine drives the electric generator, which drives the traction motors.

Driver's cab
Placed high above the engine's nose for better visibility and comfort.

CP Rail

1410

Traction motors
Drive the locomotive's wheels. One motor drives each pair of wheels.

Diesel fuel
Stored in high-capacity tanks under the engine.

Driving wheels
Two pairs per twin-axle bogie, with the pairs of axles coupled. This is the B-B configuration.

This is an EMD General Motors B-B diesel-electric driving unit. Over 60 American railroads used these 1,500-hp locomotives. One locomotive was not powerful enough to pull a large train, so the cab had an equally powerful booster unit attached behind it.

INSIDE THE DOME CAR

The Canadian has a sleek dome car near the front of the train, between its luxury coaches and the dining cars. In the dome car are 26 seats, a buffet and coffee shop, and a bar. A staircase joins the upper and lower levels of the car and allows passengers to walk up to the top of the dome to get a good view during daylight.

THE VIEW FROM THE DOME CAR

The dome car gives passengers good views of the glorious mountain scenery. Early in this century, the Canadian Pacific Railway added an open-top coach to trains passing through the mountains. Hot food and drinks were served to keep passengers warm.

OBSERVATION CAR

At the very end of the train is another domed observation car, different from the one near the front. Inside the car are three bedrooms, a drawing room, a bar under the dome, and an observation lounge. This is the best part of the train to ride in.

THE ROUTE OF THE CANADIAN

The 2,874-mile (4,636-kilometer) journey from Montreal (1) to Vancouver (4) passes beside Lake Superior before crossing the Great Plains from Winnipeg (2) to Calgary (3). The journey crosses four time zones and takes just over 71 hours – 16 hours less than before.

1410

Tube train

"A row of hard faces, immobile,
In the swaying train,
Rush across the flickering background of the fluted dingy tunnel."
Richard Aldington, "In the Tube"

LONDON TRANSPORT'S FAMOUS "ROUNDEL"

The Underground Group, which ran the London Underground, started using the "roundel" symbol in 1908 to make station names stand out from commercial advertising. It was one of the first ever company logos.

TUNNELING THROUGH CLAY

London's tube network was built underground with a machine called the Greathead Shield, invented by James Greathead in 1862. It had huge rotary cutters revolving in the circular cutting edge of the shield, which was forced slowly forward through the clay. Inside the shield, the tunnel wall bolted together from curved sections of cast iron. Modern versions of the shield are driven forward at a rate of more than 300 feet (100 meters) per day.

In 1863, the world's first underground railroad opened in London using steam locomotives. The world's first electric underground train became part of this network in 1890. Earlier underground systems had been built by digging up the street and adding a roof to make a tunnel. This method, called "cut and cover," held up traffic, and sewage pipes got in the way. New parts of London's network were dug much deeper – at 60 feet (18.3 meters), where it went below the Thames River. The work was done inside a metal tube that kept the earth from collapsing into the tunnel as the digging went on. The tunnels, 10.5 feet (3.2 meters) in diameter with cast-iron linings, gave the network the nickname "the Tube." Passengers were carried in windowless coaches. As the network grew, the tunnels got deeper. Some tunnels are 220 feet (67 meters) below ground. Huge ventilator fans provide clean air underground.

Destination panel

Emergency door

Headlight

Driver's cab

BAKER STREET

037

Wedglock mechanical coupler

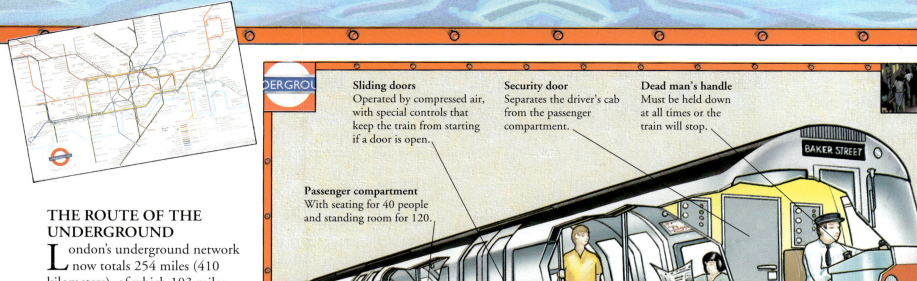

Sliding doors
Operated by compressed air, with special controls that keep the train from starting if a door is open.

Security door
Separates the driver's cab from the passenger compartment.

Dead man's handle
Must be held down at all times or the train will stop.

Passenger compartment
With seating for 40 people and standing room for 120.

Collector shoe
Slides on rails collecting 600 volts DC to power the train.

The Underground uses electric multiple-unit trains. Each coach is 52ft. 9in. (16 meters) long, 8ft. 8 in. (2.6 meters) wide and weighs 28.6 tons. A train with seven coaches has four power cars with four axles each, powered by 300 volt traction motors. The train is almost totally automatic, including braking and accelerating, with combined fail-safe brake systems.

THE ROUTE OF THE UNDERGROUND

London's underground network now totals 254 miles (410 kilometers), of which 103 miles (167 kilometers) are underground. Extending into the suburbs, 270 stations handle more than 750 million passengers a year.

DEEP-LEVEL INTERCHANGE AT PICCADILLY CIRCUS

The Piccadilly and Bakerloo lines form an important interchange station at Piccadilly Circus, London. This complicated underground station took four years to build in the 1920s and was designed to handle over five million passengers a year. Eleven reversible escalators, moving at the rate of 100 feet (30.5 meters) per minute, carry passengers down to the platforms below. The large circular booking hall, 15 feet (4.6 meters) below ground level, covers 15,000 square feet (1,394 square meters). It houses shops, the booking office and automatic ticket machines.

SHELTERING DURING THE BLITZ (1940–1941)

During World War 2, thousands of people in London used the deep-level Tube stations as shelters when German planes bombed the city. Rows of people on folding beds would spend the nights sleeping safely on the station platforms, more than 160 feet (50 meters) below the damaged streets.

Eurostar

"It's sleek to look at silky smooth to travel on and will race between European capitals at three miles a minute. In short the 'Eurostar' is as sensational as it looks."
Peter Semmens, *Railway Magazine*, June 1994

Connecting London to Paris and Brussels, Eurostar is the sleekest, fastest train in daily use in the world. In time it will connect all the main cities of Europe by high-speed rail. Eurostar made history not only for its speed but also for traveling through the new Channel Tunnel under the English Channel between England and France. This huge feat of engineering was carried out by a joint French and British company. The triple-bore tunnel, 31 miles (50 kilometers) long, was opened in May 1994 by the Queen and President François Mitterrand of France. Eurostar itself was built by a team of English, French and Belgian companies. Its design resembles the older French TGV Atlantique. Like the TGV, Eurostar regularly travels at 186 miles (299 kilometers) per hour on the new high-speed lines in France. In Britain and parts of Belgium the train still uses ordinary lines and it goes more slowly. Pneumatic suspension on the coaches gives a smooth ride even at the fastest speeds. Each Eurostar trainset has 18 coaches. No extra coaches may be added to a set. The trainset can be pushed along by the rear power car if the front power car fails. Speed is controlled by computer, and there are three types of brakes to meet safety standards in all three countries.

POWER SUPPLY

Three kinds of power supply are used on Eurostar, two of them picked up overhead by a pantograph on each car. It uses 750 volts in Britain and 3,000 volts in parts of Belgium. On the high-speed lines in France, Belgium and the Channel Tunnel, it draws 25,000 volts from overhead wires. Eventually it will use this everywhere.

LINKS WITH EUROPE

In 1995, Eurostar trains ran only from London (1) to Paris (2) and Brussels (3). New connections are planned for other European cities – Madrid, Milan and Geneva from Paris, and Amsterdam and Frankfurt from Brussels. Eventually, most of Europe will be linked by high-speed rail. Members of the European Union have already agreed to update their rail systems to join the network.

High-intensity headlight

Driver's window

Nose cone

Access panel for electrical equipment

STEPS FOR THREE DIFFERENT LEVELS

The doors of Eurostar trains have electrically operated adjustable steps. Station platforms vary from 36 inches (91.5 centimeters) in Britain to 30 inches (76.0 centimeters) in Belgium and 21.5 inches (55.0 centimeters) in France. The steps can also be lowered so that passengers can reach emergency catwalks in the Channel Tunnel.

AC pantograph
Collects electric current from overhead wire in Tunnel and from high-speed lines in Belgium and France.

Air inlet grilles
Part of the ventilation system.

Motor blocs
Two large motor blocs at the rear of the power car give power up to 12,200kw.

Air reservoir
With a capacity of 92gals. (355 liters).

Collector shoe
Collects current from the third rail in the United Kingdom.

Suspension
Coiled-spring secondary suspension.

Eurostar can carry 794 passengers. Fully loaded, it weighs 816 tons. Its traction motors build up 16,400hp, giving a top speed of 186mph (299kph). At this speed it takes one minute five seconds, and a distance of almost 2mi. (3km), to come to a complete stop. A trainset has two power cars and 18 trailer cars, totaling 1,300ft. (394m) in length.

SHUTTLE CAR TRANSPORTER

Freight, lorries and passenger cars travel on Le Shuttle, which runs on the same line as Eurostar. Le Shuttle offers a way to cross the English Channel without having to drive on or off a ferry – and it is not canceled in bad weather. One shuttle train can carry up to 120 cars, 12 coaches, and 1,000 passengers at 85 miles (137 kilometers) per hour. Passengers may stay in their cars for the journey through the Tunnel, which lasts only 35 minutes.

DRIVER'S CONSOLE

The driver's console is in the center of the cab, giving the best view of the track. Computers help the driver control the train. They also read the signals along the line, because the speed of the train often makes them go by in a blur. If the driver does not respond to signals, the train automatically slows down or stops. The console is linked to the control center in France and can check equipment inside the train. Drivers must be able to speak English and French, but they can choose either language to display information on their computers. Speed limits are displayed in miles or kilometers per hour depending on the train's location.

What is an aircraft?

An aircraft is a flying machine. Gliders, fighters, bombers, helicopters, airships and airliners are all types of aircraft. Indeed, so varied are today's aircraft and the tasks to which they are put, that it is difficult to believe that modern aviation really only began little more than 90 years ago. The fascination with flying has inspired mankind for thousands of years, and as long ago as the fifteenth century the inventor Leonardo da Vinci had designed flying machines – but it is doubtful whether they were ever built and tested.

Our story, however, begins at the start of the twentieth century when two American brothers, Wilbur and Orville Wright, made the first successful powered aircraft flight. From this achievement have come all of today's complex flying machines. In this book we look at a variety of the world's great aircraft – each one chosen because it represents a landmark in the development of flight. Because many of these aircraft were later modified, we often show more than one version to illustrate the variety of designs which were created.

FLYING THE FLAG
Many civilian and military aircraft carry badges and insignia. These are often based on a country's national colors, and are equivalent to the flags flown on ships.

HELICOPTERS
Instead of wings, helicopters have long, thin rotor blades that whirl around. The spinning rotor blades enable helicopters to take off and land vertically, so they do not need the long runways that airplanes with wings require.

CIVILIAN AIRCRAFT
Civilian aircraft are designed to carry passengers or cargo. The passenger cabins of large airliners are pressurized so that the passengers can breathe normally in the thin air high above the ground.

Canada

Russia

Italy

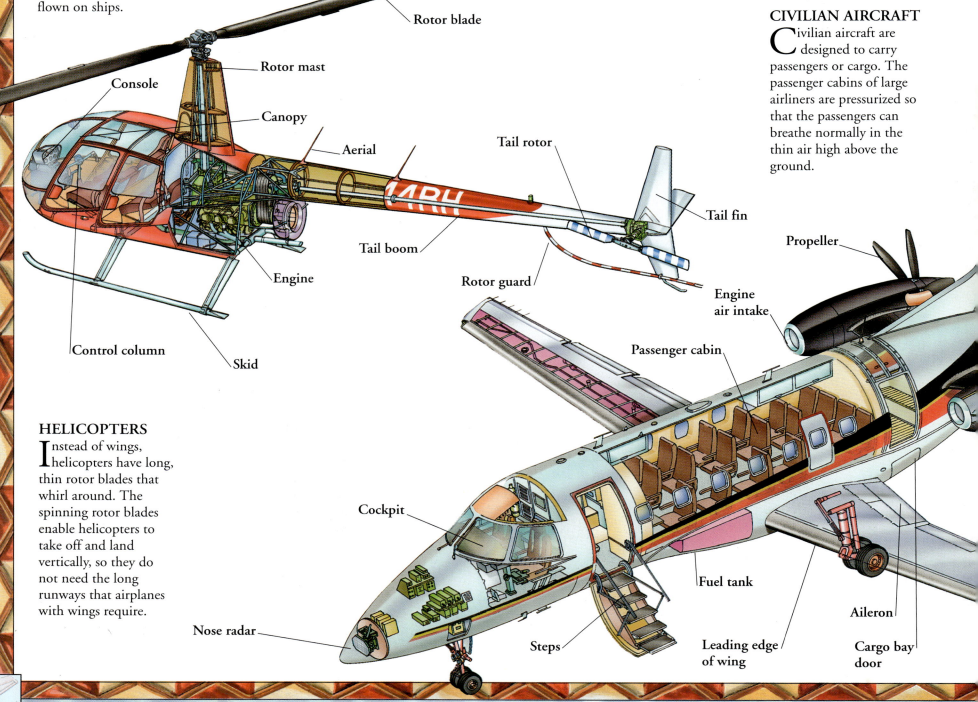

Rotor blade

Rotor mast

Console

Canopy

Aerial

Tail rotor

Tail fin

Tail boom

Engine

Rotor guard

Control column

Skid

Propeller

Engine air intake

Passenger cabin

Cockpit

Fuel tank

Aileron

Nose radar

Steps

Leading edge of wing

Cargo bay door

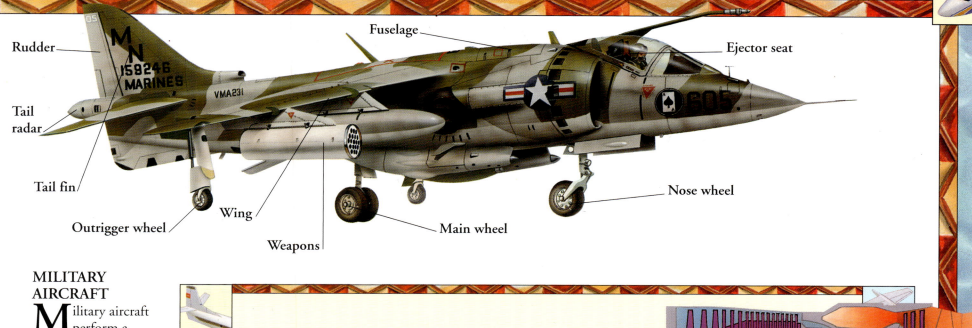

Rudder

Tail radar

Tail fin

Outrigger wheel

Wing

Weapons

Main wheel

Fuselage

Ejector seat

Nose wheel

MILITARY AIRCRAFT

Military aircraft perform a variety of different roles for armies, air forces and navies. Fighters attack other aircraft. Bombers drop bombs or fire missiles. Transport aircraft carry troops and vehicles. Reconnaissance aircraft spy on the enemy.

Elevator

Static dischargers

Exhaust nozzle

Engine

Trailing edge of wing

Navigation light

PRINCIPLES OF FLIGHT

All heavier-than-air aircraft have wings or rotor blades to lift them into the air, and all except gliders and helicopters have to be thrust forward by engines to gain lift. Craft such as airships create lift in a different way, using lighter-than-air gas.

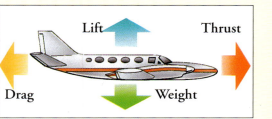

Lift

Thrust

Drag

Weight

LIFT, DRAG, THRUST, WEIGHT

Every airplane has four forces acting on it. Its engines thrust it forward while air resistance, or drag, tries to slow it down. The wings must produce enough lift to overcome its weight. The diagram on the left shows these four forces.

PITCH, ROLL, YAW

An aircraft can turn in three ways, called pitch, roll and yaw. Raising or lowering its nose is a change in pitch. Lowering one wing and raising the other makes the aircraft roll. Turning the nose to the left or right is a yaw movement. The diagram on the right shows the parts of the aircraft that are operated to make the movements occur.

WING AIRFLOW

Air flowing over the top of a wing has to travel farther and faster than air flowing under it. This makes the air pressure over the wing fall, creating an upward force called lift.

FLAPS AND SLATS

When a plane takes off or lands, slats move out in front of its wings and flaps stretch out behind them. They make the wings bigger to produce more lift when the plane is flying slowly. When it lands, spoilers lift up to "spoil" the wing's shape and reduce lift.

Roll

Yaw

Pitch

Rudder controls yaw

Elevators control pitch

Ailerons control roll

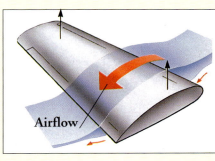

Airflow

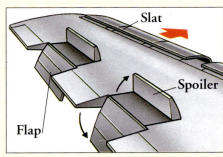

Slat

Spoiler

Flap

JET ENGINE

A spinning fan sucks air inside the engine, where fuel is sprayed into it and lit. The gases rush out of the engine as a jet, which produces thrust.

Lift

HELICOPTER

A helicopter's rotor blades are long, thin wings. As they whirl around, air flowing over them produces a force acting upward. Making the blades spin faster or changing the angle of the blades alters the lifting force. The tail rotor prevents the helicopter itself from being spun around by the action of the main rotor blade.

Development and uses of aircraft

The development of aircraft and the speed at which this has happened has been astonishing. Only 66 years separate the very first airplane and supersonic airliners. At first, a variety of purposes were achieved by a single aircraft. For example, the same plane was used for spying and dropping bombs. It became apparent, however, that one aircraft could not carry out different sorts of functions efficiently. Aircraft were therefore designed whose construction suited particular purposes. Nowadays, we have different types of planes, ranging from airliners and planes that spray crops and fight fires to bombers and spyplanes.

TAKING OFF

The chart below shows the key dates in the development of aircraft from the first plane in 1903 to the F-117A high-tech stealth fighter used today.

1940s: Avro Lancaster Bomber: the most successful bomber of World War II

1947: First supersonic flight in a Bell X-1 experimental rocket-powered plane

1930s: First long-distance civilian flying boats. These were planes that landed on water.

1936: Igor Sikorsky designed a helicopter with an overhead main rotor and a smaller tail rotor.

1930s: Development of airships. The *Hindenburg* (1936) was the largest of these.

1920s: First commercial airliner: Handley Page HP42

1903: First powered airplane: *Flyer 1*

DEVELOPMENT

Designers have constantly looked for ways of improving their aircraft. Aircraft have become safer, more comfortable and faster. As aircraft have become more specialized, so too has their design. Each new design has provided valuable experience that has led to further improvements.

Sopwith Camel pilot

"Blackbird" pilot

Flyer 1's controls

Harrier AV8-A instrument panel

FLYING CONTROLS

Cables were used to steer early planes. They were linked to the plane's control surfaces and were operated by the pilot. Nowadays, planes are too powerful and fast to be operated manually. In the latest steering system, called fly-by-wire, computers operate the plane's control surfaces.

CLOTHING

Clothing worn by pilots has become more specialized. The pilots of early planes wore leather helmets, fleece-lined leather coats, trousers and goggles. Nowadays, pilots who fly at high altitude wear pressure suits and helmets.

WINGS

The first aircraft had two pairs of wings held in place by wires and wooden struts. As airplane speed increased, the wood and wire caused too much air resistance. Modern aircraft have one pair of metal wings. The wings are swept back to reduce air resistance.

Sopwith Camel wings

Concorde "delta" wing

Harrier AV8-A engine

Flyer 1 engine

ENGINES

The first airplane engines were piston engines, similar to those in a modern car. In the 1930s, Britain and Germany both developed a new type of engine – the jet engine. Jet-engine aircraft can fly higher and faster than piston-engine planes.

1967: First aircraft capable of vertical takeoff and landing, as well as short takeoff and landing: the Harrier "Jump Jet"

1981: First stealth combat aircraft: Lockheed F-117A "Nighthawk"

1949: First jet airliner: de Havilland Comet. Entered service in 1952

1958: First transatlantic jet airliner services between London and New York with a de Havilland Comet 4

1964: First stealth aircraft: Lockheed SR-71 "Blackbird"

1969: First supersonic airliner: Concorde

USES

Aircraft are used for civilian and military purposes. They transport people and goods from place to place far more quickly than would be possible by road, rail or sea. Military aircraft are used for defense and attack. Some of them are bombers, others are fighters, others are capable of both. Some military aircraft are used for spying. Large numbers of small aircraft are also flown for leisure.

CIVILIAN AIRCRAFT

Vacations in far-away places would be impossible for most people without fast air travel. Business around the world would also be far more difficult. At first, there were very few airports. Airplanes took off from fields. Nowadays, many cities have at least one airport. The picture above shows the boarding walkway leading from the airport terminal to the aircraft.

FLYING FOR FUN

Many different types of aircraft exist that are flown for fun. Examples of these are balloons, single-seat aircraft called microlights, hang-gliders and gliders. Gliders, shown above, are first towed into the sky by another plane or by a winch on the ground, and then use rising columns of air to carry them upward.

MILITARY AIRCRAFT

Winning control of the air is a vital part of winning a war. Fighters patrol the skies ready to attack enemy aircraft. Ground-attack aircraft and bombers strike against targets on the ground. Transport aircraft carry troops, vehicles and supplies to where they are needed and reconnaissance aircraft spy on the enemy. The picture to the right shows a jeep driving out of a Boeing Vertol CH-47 Chinook.

The first flight

"Only those who are acquainted with practical aeronautics can appreciate the difficulties of attempting the first trials of a flying machine in a 25-mile gale . . . but . . . we were determined . . . to know whether the machine possessed sufficient power to fly."

Wilbur Wright's statement to *The Associated Press*, January 5, 1904

Wilbur Wright   *Orville Wright*

WRIGHT BROTHERS

The first successful airplanes were designed by two American bicycle makers; Wilbur (1867–1912) and Orville (1871–1948) Wright.

At 10:35 a.m. on December 17, 1903 *Flyer 1*, the world's first successful airplane, accelerated along its launching rail and rose into the air. Twelve seconds later, it landed 100yds. (30m) away on the soft sand at Kill Devil Hills near Kitty Hawk in North Carolina. It was the first time a piloted machine had taken off under its own power and made a controlled flight. The pilot, Orville Wright, and his brother, Wilbur, had built the plane after four years of experiments with kites and gliders. Flying the first airplane was difficult and dangerous. *Flyer 1* had no cockpit or even a seat to sit on! The pilot lay on the lower wing and steered by sliding from side to side. It landed on skids, not wheels.

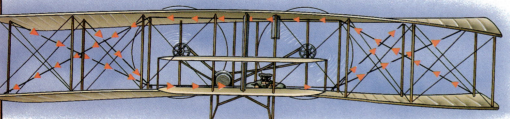

STEERING

Flyer 1 was steered by twisting its wings. The Wright brothers called it wing-warping. The wings were warped, or twisted, by pulling cables attached to them and to the cradle the pilot lay in. The pilot steered by sliding his body to one side or the other.

Upper wing

Bracing wire

TAKEOFF

While one brother piloted the plane, the other brother stayed at the takeoff point and timed the flight with a stopwatch.

ENGINEERING SUCCESS

The brothers designed their own engine because car engines were too heavy and motorcycle engines were not powerful enough. Their engine had four cylinders, weighed 200lb. (90kg) and created 12 hp – about a sixth of the engine power of a small modern car. The plane's top speed was 30mph (48kph).

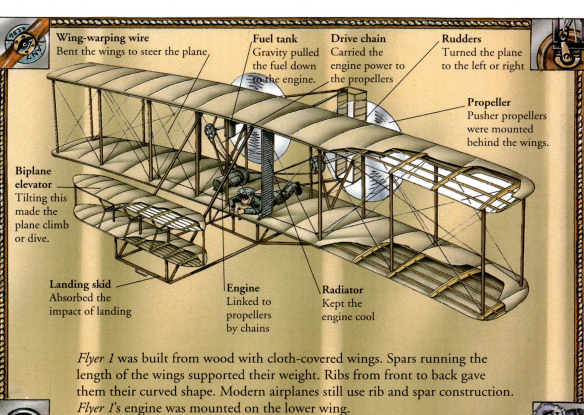

Wing-warping wire
Bent the wings to steer the plane.

Fuel tank
Gravity pulled the fuel down to the engine.

Drive chain
Carried the engine power to the propellers

Rudders
Turned the plane to the left or right

Propeller
Pusher propellers were mounted behind the wings.

Biplane elevator
Tilting this made the plane climb or dive.

Landing skid
Absorbed the impact of landing

Engine
Linked to propellers by chains

Radiator
Kept the engine cool

Flyer 1 was built from wood with cloth-covered wings. Spars running the length of the wings supported their weight. Ribs from front to back gave them their curved shape. Modern airplanes still use rib and spar construction. *Flyer 1*'s engine was mounted on the lower wing.

Wing strut

Lower wing

Cradle

THE PILOT

Flyer 1 was flown by a pilot lying in a cradle, rather like a hammock, mounted on the lower wing. The cradle was positioned to one side of the plane's center-line to balance the weight of the engine on the other side.

Canvas and string

The Sopwith Camel was built during Word War I (1914–1918) as a fighter plane, and was based on the earlier Sopwith Pup fighter. It was one of the greatest fighter aircraft of the war. At a height of 19,028ft. (5,800m) it could reach a speed of 115mph (185kph), and could fly 100mi. (160km) before it needed to be refueled. It could fly for two hours at the most. More than 5,000 were built and they shot down almost 2,800 German planes. The Camels were faster and more maneuverable than most other fighters. But they were difficult to fly. A careless tug on the joystick could send a Camel into a dangerous spin or even throw the pilot out of the cockpit. And during this time, pilots did not wear parachutes! The pilot sat in a wicker seat in front of the fuel tank. His view was restricted by the upper wing and struts.

HAND BOMBING
The Sopwith Camel carried four 24-lb. (11-kg) bombs as well as other weapons. At the beginning of the war, before the introduction of bomb racks and aiming sights, the bombs were dropped from the cockpit by the pilot.

Bracing wire

Upper wing

Rotary engine

Lower wing

Wooden propeller

Metal engine cover

AERIAL PHOTOGRAPHY
Using planes for reconnaissance purposes was a new development in warfare. Sopwith Camel pilots took aerial photographs of enemy territory (1), and the photographs were used to make maps (2). These enabled the pilots to identify targets and the position of enemy troops.

PILOTS' CLOTHING
The air temperature drops very quickly as aircraft climb. Camel pilots had to wear leather helmets and fleece-lined leather clothes on top of thick sweaters, trousers, gloves and socks. Goggles protected the pilots' eyes from cold wind and from oil sprayed out by the engine. By the end of the war, pilots wore one-piece waxed-cotton flying suits lined with silk and fur.

DOGFIGHT

During World War I, pilots on the German and the British sides became expert at dogfighting. The Sopwith Camel was especially good at this because it was so maneuverable. But the pilot with the most "hits" was the legendary German, Manfred von Richthofen, who was known as the "Red Baron" because he liked to fly a bright red Fokker triplane. He was shot down and killed by Sopwith Camels in 1918.

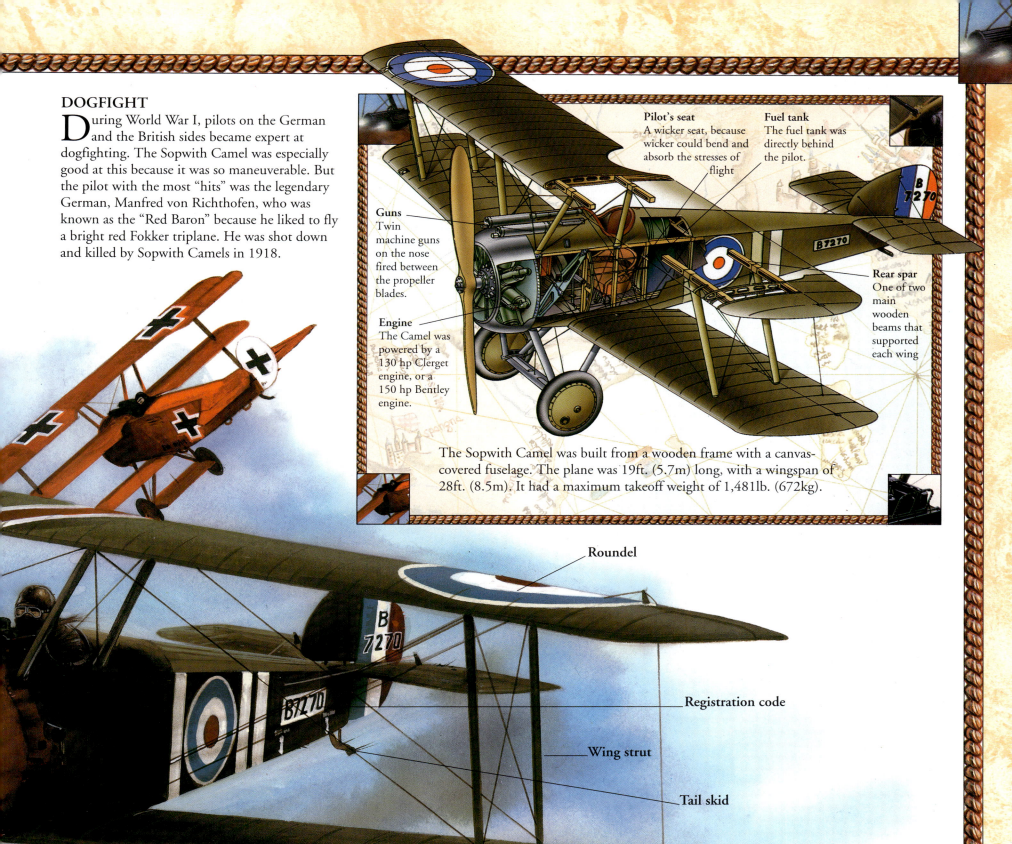

Pilot's seat
A wicker seat, because wicker could bend and absorb the stresses of flight

Fuel tank
The fuel tank was directly behind the pilot.

Guns
Twin machine guns on the nose fired between the propeller blades.

Engine
The Camel was powered by a 130 hp Clerget engine, or a 150 hp Bentley engine.

Rear spar
One of two main wooden beams that supported each wing

The Sopwith Camel was built from a wooden frame with a canvas-covered fuselage. The plane was 19ft. (5.7m) long, with a wingspan of 28ft. (8.5m). It had a maximum takeoff weight of 1,481lb. (672kg).

Roundel

Registration code

Wing strut

Tail skid

Fixed undercarriage

COCKPIT AND GUNS

Most Camels were armed with two machine guns mounted on top of the engine in front of the cockpit. The guns could not swivel, so the plane had to be turned until they pointed at their target.

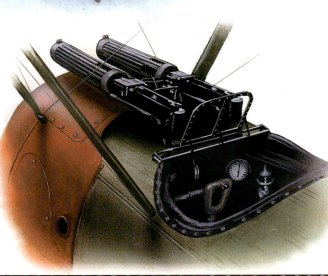

PROPELLER CANNON

The Camel below was fitted with a 1.5-in. (37-mm) Hotchkiss cannon firing through its propeller shaft. Some Camels had an extra machine gun fitted to the top wing. Others had rockets mounted on the wing struts for attacking airships.

Flying banana

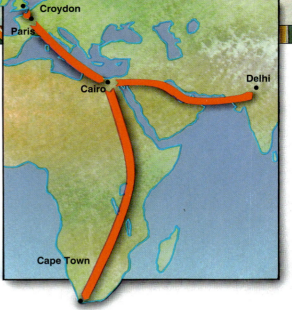

The Handley Page HP42s were nicknamed "Flying Bananas" because of the curve in their fuselage. They were designed in the late 1920s initially as special air mail planes for the British Imperial Airways airline. The HP42s also met the growing need for commercial passenger planes, and became the world's first airliners. The routes took passengers from Croydon Airport near London to France, India and southern Africa. Only eight of these biplanes were ever built. However, by the time they went out of service in 1940, they had flown a total of 9 million mi. (16 million km) without injuring a single passenger. The HP42s were designed for comfort and safety, not speed. They flew at no more than 94mph (152kph).

CROSSING CONTINENTS

The HP42 flights all took off from Croydon Airport in England. The four-hour journey to France ended at Le Bourget Airport, Paris. The six-day journey to India took passengers around the Mediterranean, through the Persian Gulf and over the sea to Pakistan. Another route flew over the Mediterranean and on to southern Africa. This took eight and a half days.

Wire bracing

Fabric wing-panel covering

Biplane tail

BOARDING PASSENGERS

Passengers boarded the HP42 through a canvas tunnel. As the plane was dedicated to the comfort and convenience of the passengers, the engines were started before they boarded to save time. The tunnel therefore shielded them from the backwash (wind) made by the propellers.

LOADING THE MAIL

Mailbags were loaded on board the HP42 at Croydon Airport. The HP42 was designed as a mail plane because Imperial Airways needed a new plane to carry air mail to India. It was one of the first planes to carry mail on international scheduled air services.

RADIO OPERATOR

Keeping contact with the ground was an important breakthrough in commercial aviation after World War I. In the HP42, a radio operator was installed behind the captain.

Engine
One of four 490 hp Bristol Jupiter engines with four-blade wooden propellers

Cockpit
Enclosed in toughened glass

Forward cabin
With 12 seats to India and southern Africa or 20 to Paris

Cargo hold
Especially designed for air mail

Galley
During long flights, the cabin staff served seven-course meals.

Rear cabin
With 12 seats to India and southern Africa or 18 to Paris

The HP42 had a length of 92ft. (28.10m) and a wingspan of 130ft. (39.62m). It could hold a maximum of 38 passengers. The engine layout was designed to cut out noise inside the plane, with two engines on the upper wing, and two engines on the lower wing.

Large observation window

Wind-driven electricity generator

INTERIORS

All passenger cabins of the HP42 looked like luxury railway carriages. Each lavishly upholstered seat was equipped with its own controls for heating and ventilation. The HP42 was thought to have the highest standards of comfort and service of any plane – equal to those of an ocean liner.

SPEED COMPARISON

The HP42 was designed for comfort and safety. It was slower than other airliners of the day, such as the Douglas DC3, and slower than some planes before it, such as the Sopwith Camel. As technology has advanced, so it has since been possible to combine speed with safety and comfort.

Concorde – 1,354mph (2,179kph)

de Havilland Comet 1 – 526mph (784kph)

Douglas DC3 – 198mph (318kph)

Sopwith Camel – 115mph (185kph)

Handley Page HP42 – 94mph (152kph)

Wright Flyer – 30mph (48kph)

Airship

Hindenburg
804ft. (245m)

Sopwith Camel
19ft. (5.7m)

Constellation
116ft. (35.4m)

Concorde
204ft. (62.1m)

SCALE

The *Hindenburg* was enormous compared with other aircraft, especially its length.

The golden age of the airship began after World War I, and was a popular form of transport until the late 1930s. The *Hindenburg* was first used in 1936, and was the largest airship ever built. It provided one of the most luxurious travel experiences there has ever been across the Atlantic. The crew were instructed to keep the nose within a five degree angle from the level position at all times, because a steeper angle would make wine bottles fall over in the dining room! However, in May 1937, as the *Hindenburg* approached its landing site in New Jersey, it burst into flames and crashed. This heralded the end of the airship era.

"A" deck

"B" deck

ACCOMMODATION

This comprised two decks: "A" and "B." The promenade deck was part of "A" deck. The accommodations included a dining room, lounge, writing room, bar and hydrogen-proof smoking room.

MOORING

While it was stationary, the *Hindenburg* was moored to a docking tower. Cables were extended from the airship's nose compartment.

Rudder

Rear engine

OBSERVATION LOUNGE

The large observation lounge with its panoramic view was a feature that no other aircraft could provide. It led off the luxurious dining room, which was big enough to serve 34 passengers in one sitting. A staff of ten to 15 stewards took care of the 50 to 70 passengers.

Central walkway
Enabled the crew to inspect the gas cells

Wire bracing
Helped to keep the gas cells rigid

Main walkway
Enabled the crew to walk the length of the airship

Gas cell
Sixteen huge cells contained 7,067,138ft.³ (200,000m³) of hydrogen-lifting gas in total.

Engine
The *Hindenburg* was powered by four diesel engines each driving a 20-ft. (6-m) long propeller.

Promenade deck
Large observation windows gave the passengers a clear view of the ground.

The *Hindenburg* was made from an aluminum alloy frame covered by thick fabric. The airship was 804ft. (245m) long and had a diameter of 134ft. (41m). It had a maximum speed of 225mph (140kph).

GETTING ON AND OFF

Passengers embarked and disembarked from the *Hindenburg* by means of two gangways that folded out from the bottom of "B" deck. A set of steps on wheels bridged the last few feet to the ground. As the airship swayed, the steps were wheeled back and forth under the end of the gangway.

Cotton-covered hull

Gondola

Promenade deck

Front engine

GONDOLA

The airship was controlled from the wheelhouse, or steering compartment, in the gondola. Only crew members had access to this. When passengers were embarking and disembarking, crutches were used to make the gondola steady. The crutches were long wooden poles with metal fittings on the ends. Attached to rails on the gondola, they stabilized the *Hindenburg* just enough for passengers to get on and off.

Australia

Singapore

India

Great
Britain

Flying boat

"I had a wonderful flight – taking off and landing in water was so smooth and fast! My journey to Marseilles was rather chilly, but the steward brought us blankets and a hot drink. I landed in Australia, two weeks after leaving England, wishing my adventure could begin all over again."
Lady Geraldine Marshall, on her arrival in Australia with Qantas Empire Airways flying boat

SERVING FOOD
The Empire flying boat was equipped with a galley, or kitchen, where simple meals and drinks were prepared. At a cruising height of 4,920ft. (1,500m), the aircraft could be shaken by sudden rough weather, making it difficult to serve meals and uncomfortable to eat them.

FLAGS
When the plane landed and became a boat, it often flew flags in the same way as a boat. The national flags of countries the plane visited or the merchant navy red ensign were raised above the cockpit.

Flying boats reached the peak of their development in the 1930s, and were the most comfortable and spacious passenger planes of the time. Their boat-like hulls and under-wing floats enabled them to operate from the sea, lakes and rivers at a time when there were few airports. Flying boats flew all the way to the Far East, making stops in dozens of strange and exotic places and taking about two weeks to get there. The Short S-23 "C" Class Empire flying boat was designed by the British aircraft company, Short Brothers. The first of this class, *Canopus,* had its maiden flight on July 4, 1936. It was bigger, faster and more powerful than other flying boats. It carried airmail bags, freight and 24 passengers.

THE EMPIRE ROUTE
Passengers boarded their flying boat at Southampton on the south coast of England. From there, they flew along the route shown on the map (left) to Sydney, Australia. The return fare was almost $400.00.

GETTING ON AND OFF
Passengers boarded their flying boat from a jetty, or floating walkway, to which the plane was moored. In the course of their journey to the other side of the world, they had to make frequent landings so that the plane could be refueled. Each time it touched down, the passengers were taken ashore by launch for a meal or an overnight stay in a nearby hotel.

Navigation light

International identification number

All-metal wing

PROMENADE CABIN

Ocean-going liners often had a promenade deck where passengers could walk around and enjoy the view. The Empire flying boats competed directly with these liners and so they tried to offer a similar level of comfort and facilities. They had a roomy promenade cabin that enabled passengers to walk around and enjoy a spectacular bird's-eye view. They could see the ground below through observation ports.

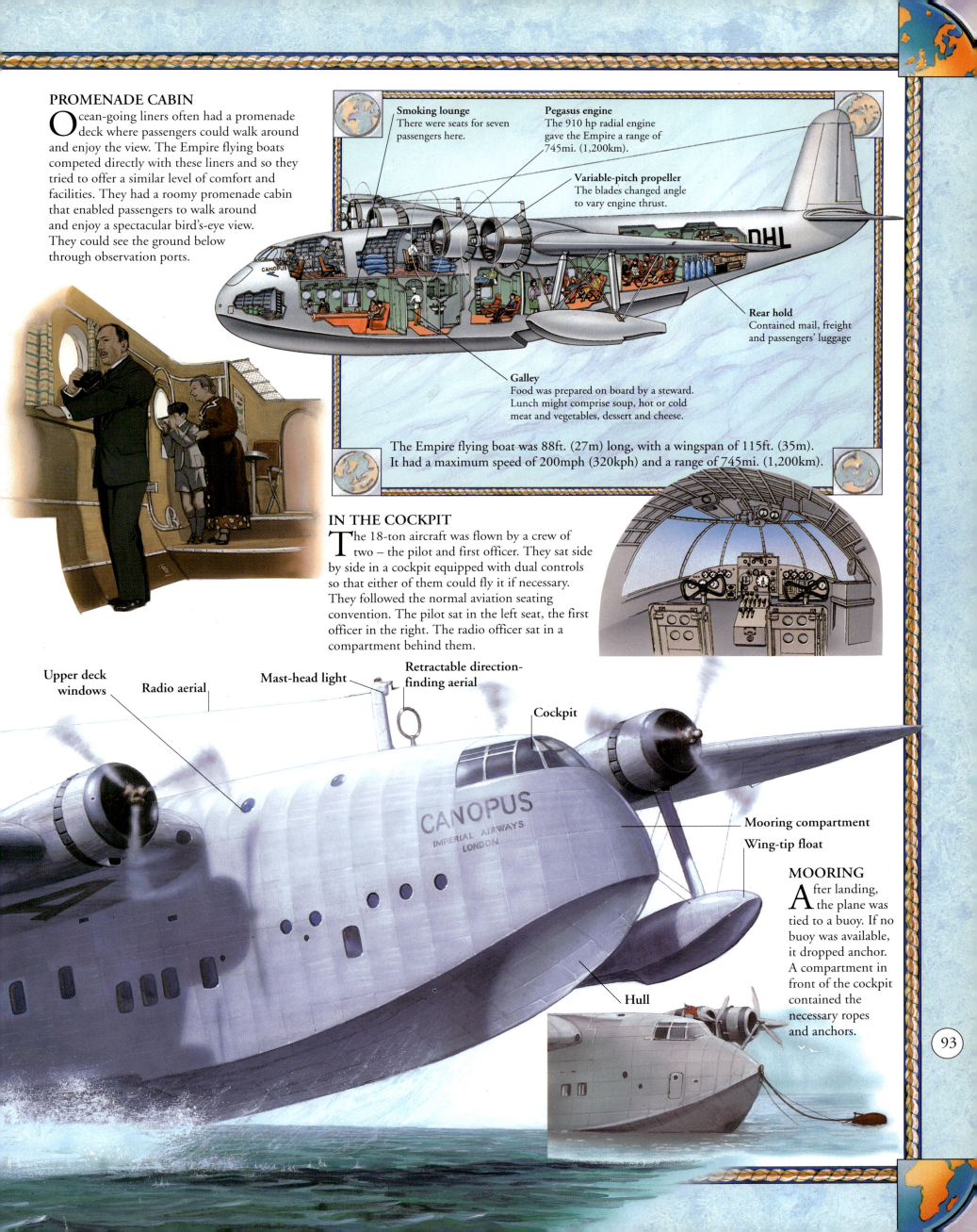

Smoking lounge
There were seats for seven passengers here.

Pegasus engine
The 910 hp radial engine gave the Empire a range of 745mi. (1,200km).

Variable-pitch propeller
The blades changed angle to vary engine thrust.

Rear hold
Contained mail, freight and passengers' luggage

Galley
Food was prepared on board by a steward. Lunch might comprise soup, hot or cold meat and vegetables, dessert and cheese.

The Empire flying boat was 88ft. (27m) long, with a wingspan of 115ft. (35m). It had a maximum speed of 200mph (320kph) and a range of 745mi. (1,200km).

IN THE COCKPIT

The 18-ton aircraft was flown by a crew of two – the pilot and first officer. They sat side by side in a cockpit equipped with dual controls so that either of them could fly it if necessary. They followed the normal aviation seating convention. The pilot sat in the left seat, the first officer in the right. The radio officer sat in a compartment behind them.

Upper deck windows

Radio aerial

Mast-head light

Retractable direction-finding aerial

Cockpit

CANOPUS
IMPERIAL AIRWAYS
LONDON

Mooring compartment

Wing-tip float

MOORING

After landing, the plane was tied to a buoy. If no buoy was available, it dropped anchor. A compartment in front of the cockpit contained the necessary ropes and anchors.

Hull

Timeless transporter

"Certainly the most famous airliner in aviation history, large numbers remain in civil and military service . . . "
Michael Taylor and David Mondey,
Guinness Book of Aircraft, Facts and Feats, 1970

The Douglas DC-3 is the most successful commercial airliner ever built. Since the first one came into service in 1936, more than 13,000 have been produced, and some are still flying today. Each aircraft could carry up to 32 passengers, depending on the seating layout. Although the DC-3 had an unladen weight of 17,703lb. (8,030kg), it could travel at up to 198mph (318kph). The DC-3 entered airline service in 1936 as a sleeper aircraft. It was so successful that by 1939, 90 percent of the world's airline passengers were carried in DC-3s. They were flown by a crew of two, with a stewardess to look after the passengers. Although the DC-3 was built originally as a civilian aircraft, most DC-3s were military versions built during World War II (1939–1945). After the war, these were bought up by airlines. One type of DC-3, the C-47, was called the "Dakota." Since then, all versions have been known as Dakotas.

FLIGHT ATTENDANT

When the DC-3 came into service, uniformed flight attendants, or stewardesses as they were known then, were still a new part of air travel. They replaced the uniformed chefs and waiters that were carried on earlier aircraft. The stewardess shown above is wearing a nurse's uniform to show that she has proper nursing qualifications.

Voice-communications radio aerial

4·21

PARACHUTISTS

Paratroops were carried on military versions of the DC-3 during World War II. Lines attached to their parachute packs were hooked on to cables inside the plane. These pulled the parachutes open when the troops jumped out.

SLEEPING COMPARTMENT

The first version of the DC-3 was the sleeper, the DST (Douglas Sleeper Transport). It was the only one of its kind at the time. The DST carried 14 passengers in berths on overnight flights. Sleeping berths are no longer on aircraft.

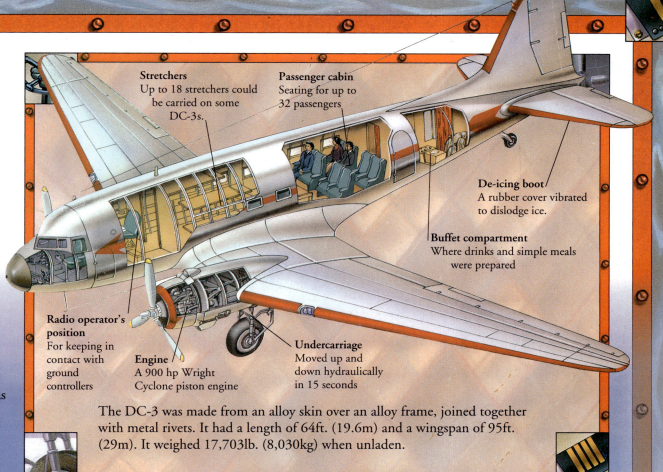

Stretchers
Up to 18 stretchers could be carried on some DC-3s.

Passenger cabin
Seating for up to 32 passengers

De-icing boot
A rubber cover vibrated to dislodge ice.

Buffet compartment
Where drinks and simple meals were prepared

Radio operator's position
For keeping in contact with ground controllers

Engine
A 900 hp Wright Cyclone piston engine

Undercarriage
Moved up and down hydraulically in 15 seconds

The DC-3 was made from an alloy skin over an alloy frame, joined together with metal rivets. It had a length of 64ft. (19.6m) and a wingspan of 95ft. (29m). It weighed 17,703lb. (8,030kg) when unladen.

Unpressurized passenger compartment

Direction-finding radio aerial

Retractable undercarriage

Ski for landing on snow

SPEEDING UP

Aircraft speeds constantly increased as new aircraft were developed. Higher speeds were achieved by using more powerful engines and building planes more streamlined in shape.

Empire Flying Boat 200mph (320kph)

Constellation 373mph (600kph)

Concorde 1,354mph (2,179kph)

DC-3 198mph (318kph)

HP42 94mph (152kph)

Hindenburg 225mph (140kph)

Wright Flyer 30mph (48kph)

A fearsome fighter

The German Messerschmitt Bf109 was developed in the 1930s by Willy Messerschmitt. It became one of the fastest, most maneuverable and well-armed fighters of World War II. Approximately 35,000 were built – more than any other fighter. It had a special system for supplying fuel to the engine, enabling it to perform maneuvers which were impossible for

other aircraft. The fastest version of the Bf109 could fly at up to 398mph (640kph) and could reach a maximum height of 36,090ft. (11,000m). It was a very popular aircraft with German pilots. They flew it high and fast, ready to accelerate to combat-speed and pounce on enemy fighters, or sweep down to attack slow-flying bombers. The Bf109's main fault was that it could not carry much fuel. It could only fly 410mi. (660km) without refueling. With such a short range, the plane was not able to linger for very long in the important combat zone over southern England.

GROUND WAR ROOM

The routes of German bombers and their fighter escorts, which protected them, were plotted on a map in the huge Berlin war room. The commanders then knew exactly how many aircraft were in action, and their positions. Many escorts were made up of Bf109s. German bomber crews believed that the Bf109s protected them more effectively than any other fighter aircraft.

Three-blade variable pitch propeller

Machine gun

PROPELLER GUN

Two 0.5-in. (13-mm) machine guns on top of the nose gun fired between the propeller blades. A 0.8-in. (20-mm) gun fired through the propeller hub. Different versions of the aircraft were armed in different ways. Some had a 0.8-in. (20-mm) cannon firing through the leading edge of each wing. It was important to keep the ammunition clean because dirt could easily jam the guns.

Retractable undercarriage

Wing cannon

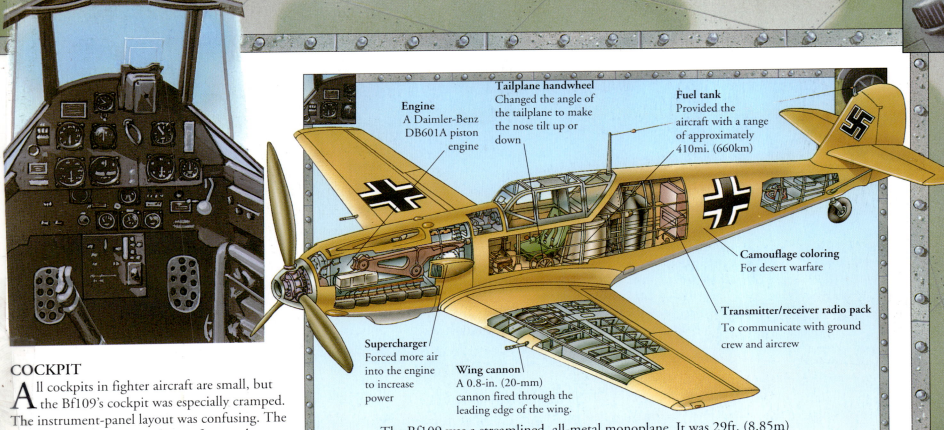

Engine
A Daimler-Benz DB601A piston engine

Tailplane handwheel
Changed the angle of the tailplane to make the nose tilt up or down

Fuel tank
Provided the aircraft with a range of approximately 410mi. (660km)

Camouflage coloring
For desert warfare

Transmitter/receiver radio pack
To communicate with ground crew and aircrew

Supercharger
Forced more air into the engine to increase power

Wing cannon
A 0.8-in. (20-mm) cannon fired through the leading edge of the wing.

The Bf109 was a streamlined, all-metal monoplane. It was 29ft. (8.85m) long, with a wingspan of 32ft. (9.9m). It had an unladen weight of 6,834lb. (3,100kg) and flew up to 398mph (640kph).

COCKPIT

All cockpits in fighter aircraft are small, but the Bf109's cockpit was especially cramped. The instrument-panel layout was confusing. The instruments that were used most frequently were not in the easiest position for the pilot to see. The foot pedals on the Bf109's cockpit floor controlled the plane's rudder. A thick cockpit frame restricted the pilot's view.

Hinged canopy

Radio aerial

FIGHTER PLANE NUMBERS

During World War II, almost 100,000 British and German fighter aircraft were built. The graph to the right shows which fighters were built, and how many of them.

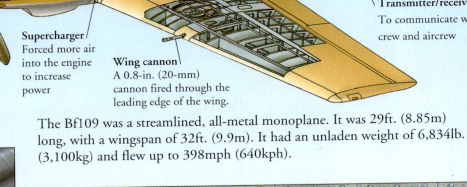

Messerschmitt Bf110	6,000
Hawker Hurricane	14,000
Focke-Wulf 190	20,000
Spitfire	20,000
Messerschmitt Bf109	35,000

British Royal Air Force 34,000   German Air Force 61,000

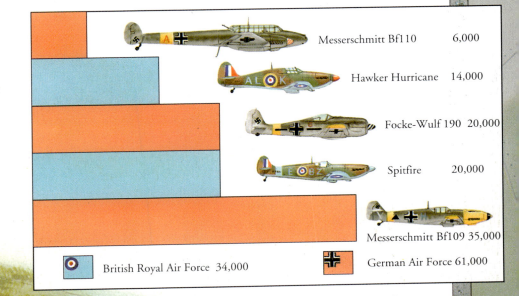

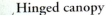

Bombs away

"The Lancaster was a thoroughbred. It looked magnificent on the ground – strong and well-proportioned. And it was powerful and well-balanced in the air. The ground crews worked their hearts out to keep us flying. The riggers and fitters, the electricians, mechanics and armorers, they all took a pride in their aircraft."
Norman Mitchell, a Lancaster bomb aimer

EMBLEMS

Each bomber crew tried to make its aircraft a little different from all the others. They gave the aircraft a name and painted a colorful emblem on its nose. This one shows a lion (a symbol of Britain) eating a German flag.

The British Avro Lancaster was one of the most successful heavy bombers of World War II. More than 7,300 were built. It flew 156,318 bombing missions, and dropped a total of 618,000 tons of bombs. It could carry a heavier bomb, and at a higher altitude, than any similar aircraft and was very maneuverable for its large size. Flying a Lancaster was a physically demanding job. The crew flew to an altitude of 21,982 ft. (6,700m) for up to 12 hours. They had to breathe oxygen through a face mask often in temperatures as low as 23°F (-5°C). The Lancasters rarely had fighter escorts, and flew mostly at night to avoid being attacked.

MISSION MARKERS

Bomber crews kept a tally of the number of missions they flew by painting a bomb on the aircraft's nose for each mission, which was called a sortie. This Lancaster has flown 47 sorties. Some flew more than 100. Most missions took place at night, when enemy fighter planes could not operate so successfully.

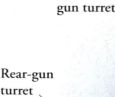

Mid-upper gun turret

Rear-gun turret

Twin-fin tail

BOMB LOADING

Heavy bombs were driven to a Lancaster on a train of trailers pulled by a tractor. The bombs were then lifted up on to racks inside the bomb bay. The 33-ft. (10-m) long bomb bay could carry different bomb loads. When loaded, the plane took a long time to take off due to the weight.

BOMB STATISTICS

As the war progressed, larger bombs were produced. The doors of the bomb bay were therefore adapted so that they curved outward to carry the bombs.

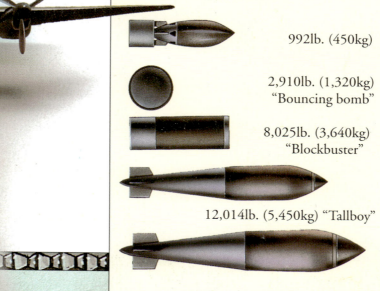

992lb. (450kg)

2,910lb. (1,320kg) "Bouncing bomb"

8,025lb. (3,640kg) "Blockbuster"

12,014lb. (5,450kg) "Tallboy"

22,046lb. (10,000kg) "Grand Slam"

FLIGHT PLANS AND LOG BOOKS

About three hours before a mission, the crew attended a briefing where they were told what their target for that night was to be. The outward and return routes were plotted on a map, or flight plan. Pilots kept a careful record of all their missions in a log book.

Engine
One of four 1,460 hp Rolls-Royce Merlin piston engines

Tail guns
Four machine guns protected the aircraft's tail.

Ammunition boxes
Supplied ammunition to the gun turrets

Fuel tanks
These enabled the plane to fly 1,730mi. (2,784km) with a bomb load of 12,000lb. (5,443kg).

Machine guns
Two 0.3-in. (7.7-mm) machine guns in nose turret

Bomb aimer's position
Bomb aimer also fired the front gun

Dark underside camouflage
Helped conceal the plane from the ground on night-flying missions

The Lancaster had a length of 70ft. (21.2m), a wingspan of 102ft. (31.1m), and a maximum takeoff weight of 72,000lb. (32,659kg). Its powerful Rolls-Royce Merlin engines gave it a maximum speed of 286mph (460kph) at a height of 21,982ft. (6,700m).

Camouflage colors

Front-gun turret

Bomb aimer's window

Bomb bay (open)

LANCASTER CREW

The Lancaster had a crew of seven. They wore up to seven layers of clothing to keep warm during the flight.

1. Wireless operator 2. Front gunner/bomb aimer 3. Flight engineer 4. Navigator 5. Pilot 6. Central gunner 7. Rear gunner

Queen of the airways

"The Constellations have more new features than any other airliner in a decade. They add up to greater speed, a higher degree of safety, more comfort and bigger and better menus."
Norman Ellison, *Sydney Sun*, 1947

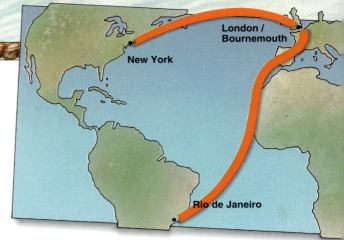

TRANSCONTINENTAL ROUTES

The Constellation helped to open the post-war long-range air routes. Transcontinental services began in 1946 with flights between New York and Bournemouth, and London and Rio de Janeiro.

The Lockheed Constellation was first developed in 1938 as a commercial airliner, but the planes were taken over by the United States Army during World War II. After the war, the Constellation was developed as a long-haul airliner for commercial flights. It was the first of the post-war airliners and was extensively developed to make long flights more attractive with its extra passenger comfort. Over the years there were many improvements on the first type of Constellation, although its drooping nose and upswept tail remained the same. Super Constellations developed, which had a fuselage that was longer, but a wingspan that remained the same. After this, came "Starliners". These had a fuselage and wings that were longer than those of the Super Constellation. Inside the aircraft, each version of the Constellation introduced new standards in passenger service. A comfortable reclining sleeper seat was first used in an Air Ceylon Constellation in 1956. The elegant Constellation was used until the late 1970s. The aircraft shown on the right is the 1049G, which was a Super Constellation. There were 26 versions of the Constellation and 49 versions of the Super Constellation.

Triple-fin tail

Upswept tail

De-icing strip

Wing-tip fuel tank

RADAR

In the 1950s the first Super Constellations used in the United States Air Force were transferred from the navy and refitted with a rotating radar dish called a rotodome, shown above. Airborne radar detects enemy planes further away than radar on the ground.

LANDING GEAR

Almost all airliners before the Constellation had a main wheel under each wing and one under the tail. The Constellation had a "tricycle" undercarriage; the wheels were arranged with one at the front and one under each wing, so the passenger cabin was parallel to the ground.

COCKTAIL LOUNGE

Lockheed spent $1,500,000.00 and 120,000 working hours giving the Super Constellation the most luxurious interior of any large passenger aircraft. The cocktail lounge had special lighting effects and peaceful color schemes to make it more relaxing.

Sleeping berths
Constellations could be fitted with up to 22 sleeping berths.

Turbo-compound engine
Four 3,250 hp turbo-supercharged engines powered the "Starliner" and Super Constellation. The first Constellations were powered by 2,300 hp piston engines.

Nosewheel
Retracted backward up into the nose

Main undercarriage
Retracted forward up into the wings

The Constellation shown here is a 1649A, also known as the "Starliner." The Constellation was 95ft. (29m) long, with a wingspan of 123ft. (37.5m). Super Constellations were 114ft. (34.6m) long with a wingspan of 123ft. (37.5m). This "Starliner" model was 116ft. (35.4m) long with a wingspan of 150ft. (45.7m). It had a maximum speed of 373mph (600kph).

Wright R-3350 Turbo-compound engine

SPEEDPAK

The Constellation could not carry much luggage. Lockheed solved this by designing a freight container, called a Speedpak, which could be attached to the aircraft's belly. A built-in electric hoist lowered the Speedpak to the ground for loading and unloading. It doubled the amount of luggage that could be loaded on to the Constellation.

Higher and faster

G·ALYT

"The Comet was years ahead of the competition, pioneering jet transportation high above the weather, and achieving journey times half that expected with piston-engined aircraft."
Philip J. Birtles, *Classic Civil Aircraft 3: de Havilland Comet*, 1993

Research into faster military aircraft during World War II speeded up the development of jet engines. At the end of the war, work began on developing jet airliners. The first jet airliner to enter service was the British de Havilland Comet 1 in 1952. It was popular with passengers because it was able to fly higher and faster than any piston-engined airliner. Shorter flights to faraway places, higher above stormy weather, were less tiring and stressful for the passengers. Comets could reach Singapore in 25 hours, or Tokyo in 36 hours. These journeys would have taken almost twice as long in a Super Constellation! But the Comet 1 had its problems, from which all aircraft manufacturers learned. The aircraft was grounded in 1954 after a series of crashes. Investigators found that the greater difference in air pressure between the inside and outside of the high-flying airplane put extra stress on the fuselage, which eventually cracked open in flight. The aircraft was strengthened and enlarged as the Comet 4, shown here, which entered service in 1958.

STRESS ANALYSIS

Following three crashes of the Comet, scientists searched for any fault that might have caused the accidents. The scientists had a Comet sealed inside a pressurized water tank to simulate the stresses of flight. In tests, the fuselage cracked open. The Comet's fuselage was strengthened and the problem ended.

GALLEY

During the flight, two stewards and a stewardess served meals and drinks. They prepared refreshments in a small galley situated just behind the flight deck. Galleys were not new to passenger aircraft. However, in-flight services became more important with the development of jet airliners.

Radio aerial (inside top of tail fin)

Pressurized passenger cabin

Rudder

Instrument Landing System aerial (inside tips of tail plane)

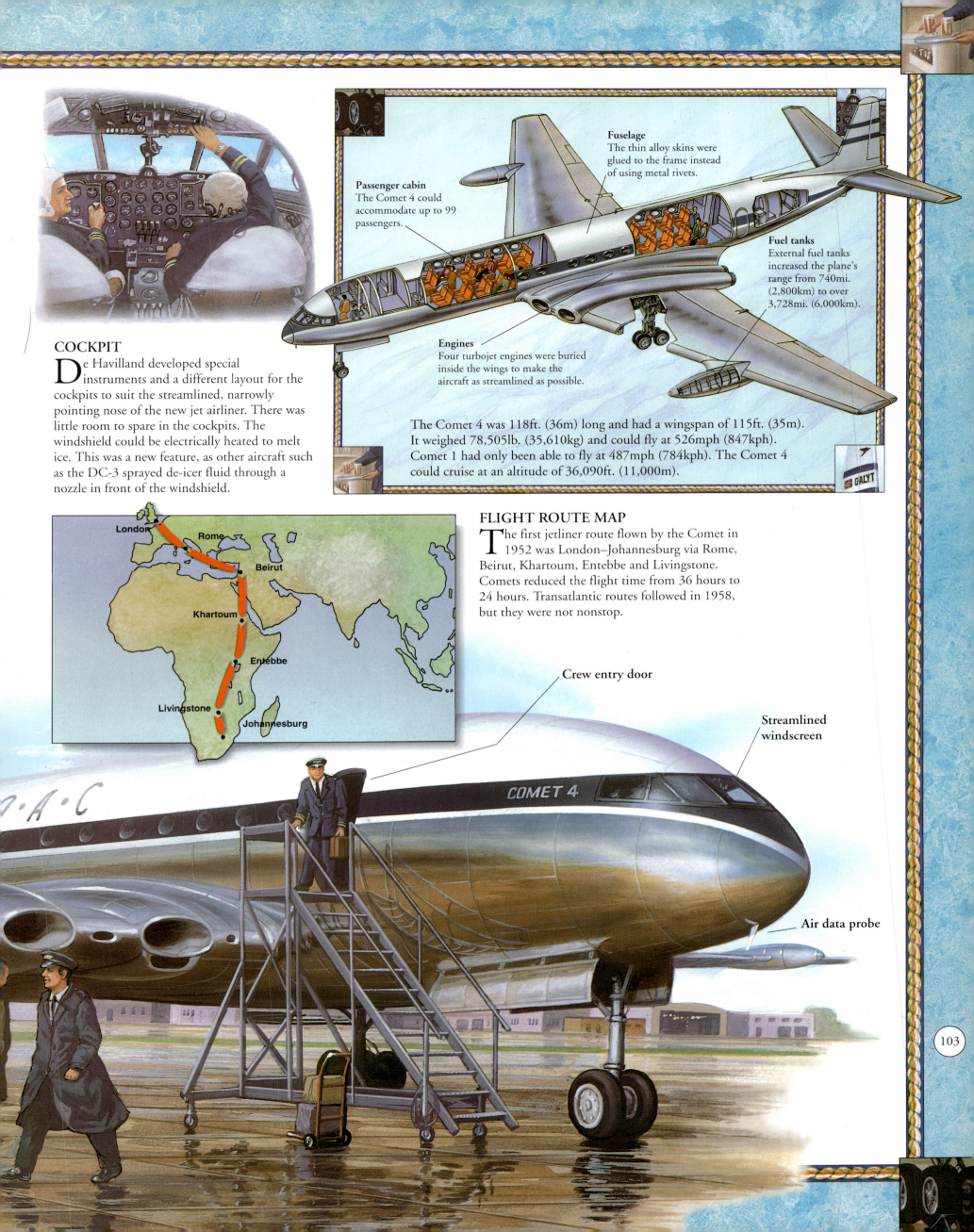

Fuselage
The thin alloy skins were glued to the frame instead of using metal rivets.

Passenger cabin
The Comet 4 could accommodate up to 99 passengers.

Fuel tanks
External fuel tanks increased the plane's range from 740mi. (2,800km) to over 3,728mi. (6,000km).

Engines
Four turbojet engines were buried inside the wings to make the aircraft as streamlined as possible.

COCKPIT

De Havilland developed special instruments and a different layout for the cockpits to suit the streamlined, narrowly pointing nose of the new jet airliner. There was little room to spare in the cockpits. The windshield could be electrically heated to melt ice. This was a new feature, as other aircraft such as the DC-3 sprayed de-icer fluid through a nozzle in front of the windshield.

The Comet 4 was 118ft. (36m) long and had a wingspan of 115ft. (35m). It weighed 78,505lb. (35,610kg) and could fly at 526mph (847kph). Comet 1 had only been able to fly at 487mph (784kph). The Comet 4 could cruise at an altitude of 36,090ft. (11,000m).

FLIGHT ROUTE MAP

The first jetliner route flown by the Comet in 1952 was London–Johannesburg via Rome, Beirut, Khartoum, Entebbe and Livingstone. Comets reduced the flight time from 36 hours to 24 hours. Transatlantic routes followed in 1958, but they were not nonstop.

London
Rome
Beirut
Khartoum
Entebbe
Livingstone
Johannesburg

Crew entry door

Streamlined windscreen

COMET 4

Air data probe

Mighty monster

"Loading and preflight checks took 45 minutes. We normally took a ten-minute break before engine start to get the sweat out of our suits or we'd freeze at altitude."
Captain Don Jansky, B-52 pilot

The American B-52 Stratofortress was first designed in the mid-1940s as a heavy bomber. It developed in the 1950s as a long-range nuclear bomber because World War II had shown that the long-range heavy bomber was the most threatening weapon available to attack an enemy's territory. The huge aircraft is known affectionately by its crews as the "Buff," the Big Ugly Fat Fella. It has never dropped a nuclear bomb, but it has been used for non-nuclear bombing.

Its crew enters the aircraft through a small hatch in its belly. The aircraft commander and copilot fly the plane from their side-by-side seats in the cockpit. Behind them, facing backward, sits the defensive team of electronic warfare officers. One of them also operates the tail gun.

Early B-52 crews wore an uncomfortable skin-tight pressure suit. It inflated automatically if the cabin pressure was lost. Later, B-52s were flown at much lower altitudes to avoid detection by enemy radar. Pressure suits then became unnecessary.

The "Buff" has lasted a long time because it has been updated regularly. Different versions of the latest model of the B-52 exist, including reconnaissance versions. The B-52 can hold many different combinations of weapons. It is the world's heaviest bomber, and can carry up to 99,206lb. (45,000kg) of bombs.

TAIL GUN

The B-52's only defensive armament is in its tail. The model shown here has a six-barrelled machine gun. Early models were armed with four machine guns.

Turbofan engines

Stratotanker

REFUELING

In-flight refueling means that the B-52 can travel virtually any distance. Lights underneath the tanker aircraft guide the B-52 into the correct position for refueling.

ENGINE

All B-52 Stratofortresses except for the latest model, the B-52H, were powered by eight turbojets, grouped in four pairs. The B-52H is powered by eight turbofans, like the one shown here, because these are quieter and use less fuel than turbojets. They also increase power performance dramatically, allowing the aircraft to take off quickly. These engines can run for 4,000 hours before needing a service – the older turbojets could run for only 500 hours between services.

TAKING OFF

The chart below compares the maximum takeoff weight of the B-52 with that of other aircraft in this book.

B-52H Stratofortress   487,992lb. (221,353kg)

Avro Lancaster B-1   72,000lb. (32,659kg)

Lockheed F-117A   52,500lb. (23,814kg)

Sopwith Camel   1,481lb. (672kg)

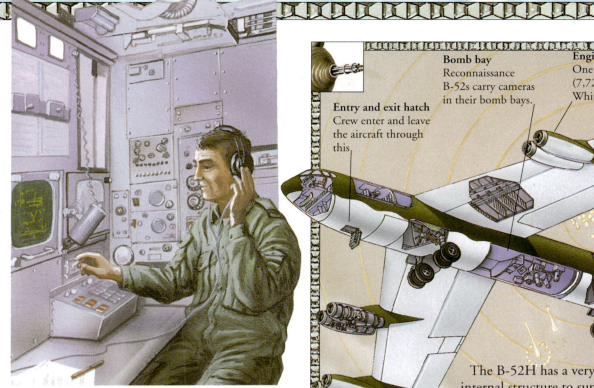

Bomb bay
Reconnaissance B-52s carry cameras in their bomb bays.

Engine
One of eight 17,019lb. (7,720kg) Pratt and Whitney turbofans

Entry and exit hatch
Crew enter and leave the aircraft through this

Outrigger wheel
Supports the wing tips when the aircraft is on the ground

Main wheels
Swivel up into fuselage after takeoff

Tail fin
A narrow rudder runs the full height of the huge tail fin.

The B-52H has a very strong internal structure to support its engines and wings full of fuel. Its maximum speed is 595mph (958kph) at a height of 55,774ft. (17,000m). The plane has a length of 161ft. (49.04m) and weighs up to 487,992lb. (221,353kg) at takeoff.

NAVIGATION

The two radar navigators sit behind and below the cockpit, facing forward. They are beneath the electronic warfare officers. Their seats eject downward through the belly of the aircraft.

Low-light television camera

Forward Looking Infra-Red (FLIR) viewing system

Under-wing fuel tank

LOADING MISSILES

Cruise missiles are loaded on to pylons under a B-52's wings. Once they are safely loaded, their explosive warheads are plugged into the empty bays at the front of the missiles.

Whirlybird

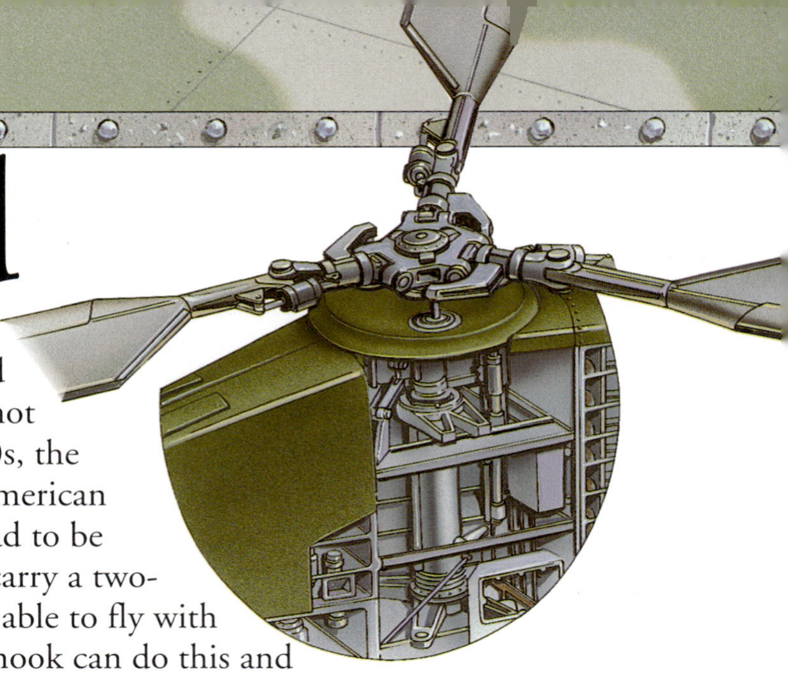

The first helicopters were not very strong and could not carry a heavy load, so they were not suited to military requirements. But in the 1950s, the Boeing-Vertol CH-47 Chinook answered the American Army's need for a very powerful helicopter. It had to be one that could transport at least 40 troops and carry a two-ton load inside it. The helicopter also had to be able to fly with an eight-ton load slung underneath it. The Chinook can do this and more. It has become a valuable multipurpose air-truck for transporting troops and equipment. Military forces all over the world use this helicopter. Two sets of controls allow either the pilot or copilot, sitting side by side, to fly the aircraft. The Chinook, like most modern helicopters, is powered by turboshaft jet engines. These are fitted at the rear of the aircraft and linked to the rotor blades by spinning shafts. Noise and vibration from the rotor blades are so great that the crew talk to each other through intercoms.

"By 1969 American Army Chinooks had flown a total of half a million hours – more than two thirds of them under combat conditions in Korea . . . The Chinook forms part of America's heavy brigade."
Robert Jackson, *The Dragonflies*
1971

Rear rotor
Textron Lycoming T55-L-712 turboshaft engine
Radio aerial
US ARMY 981143
ARMY
Cargo ramp
Main cargo hook

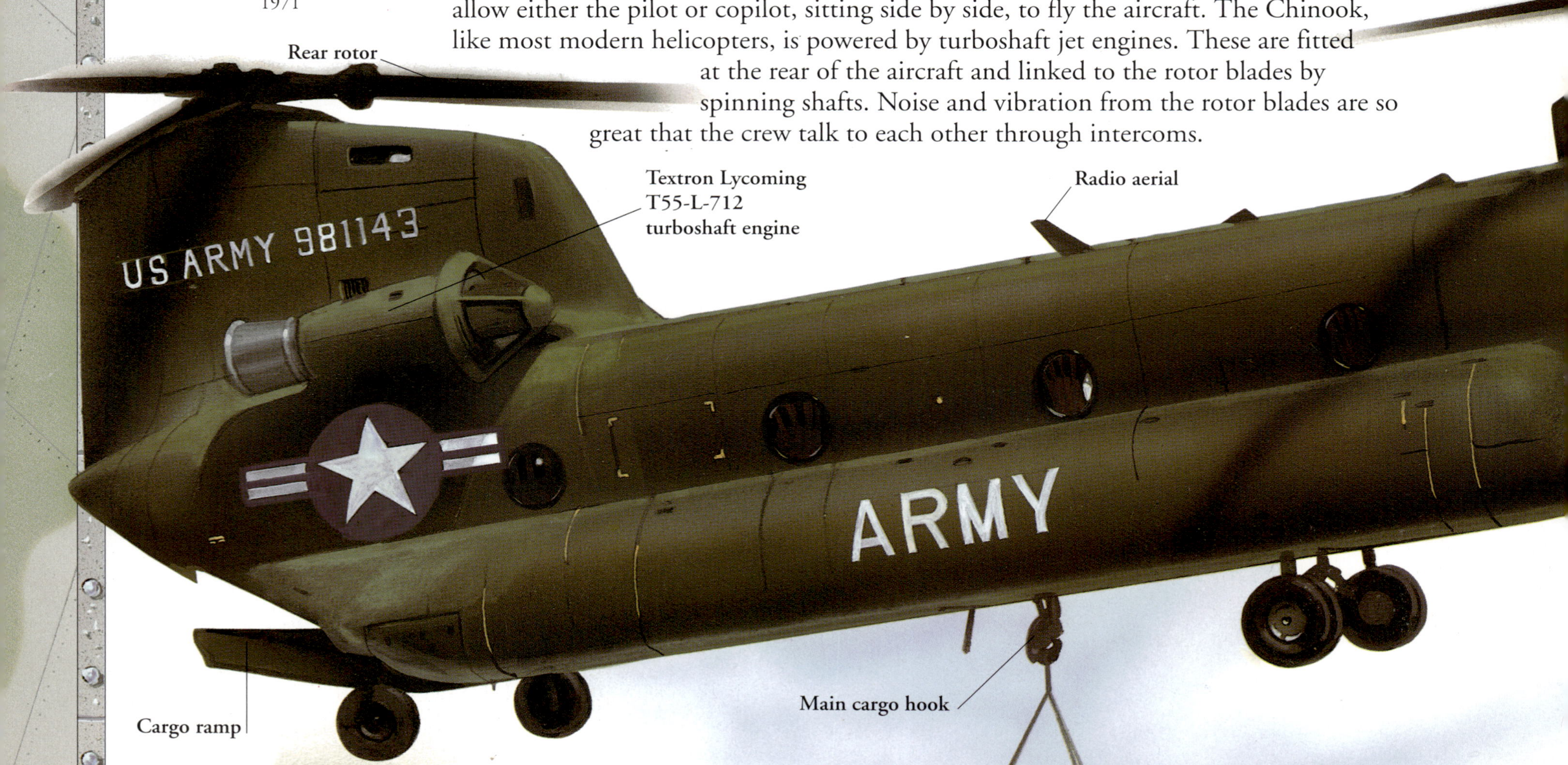

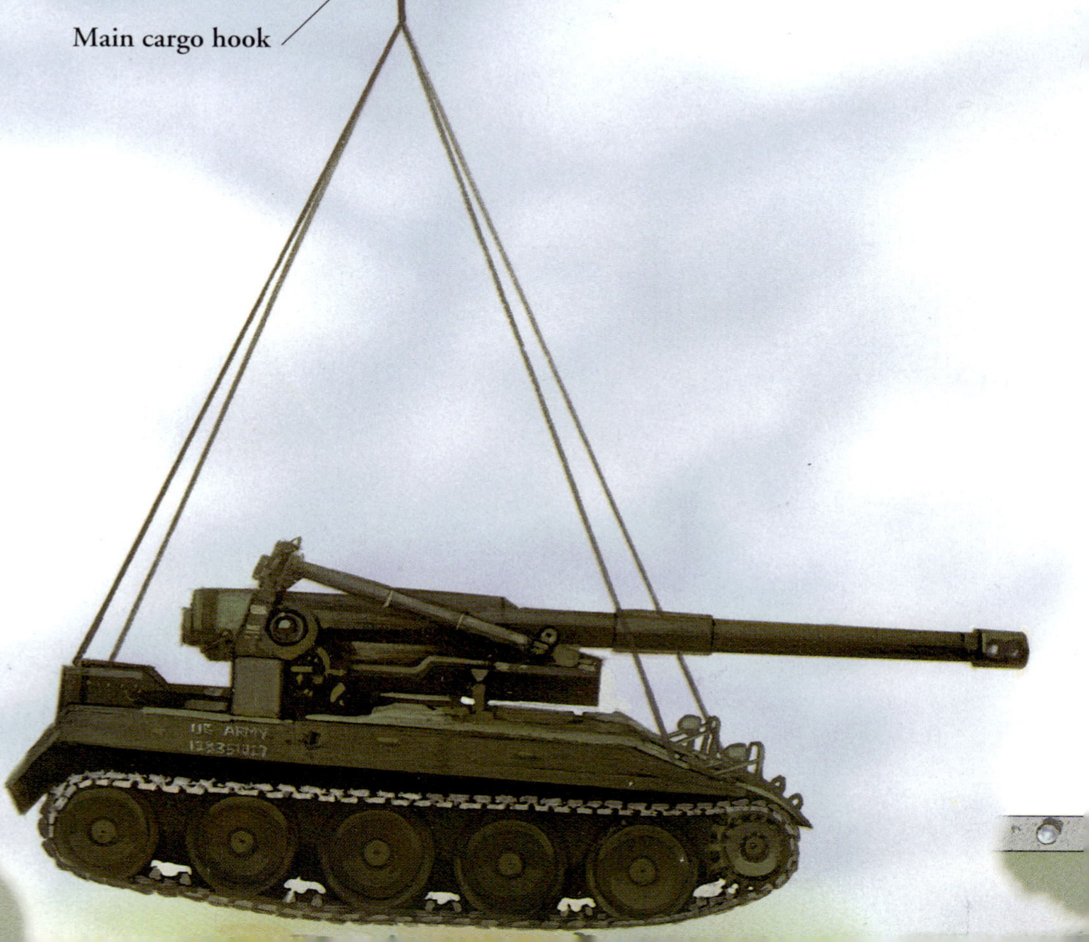

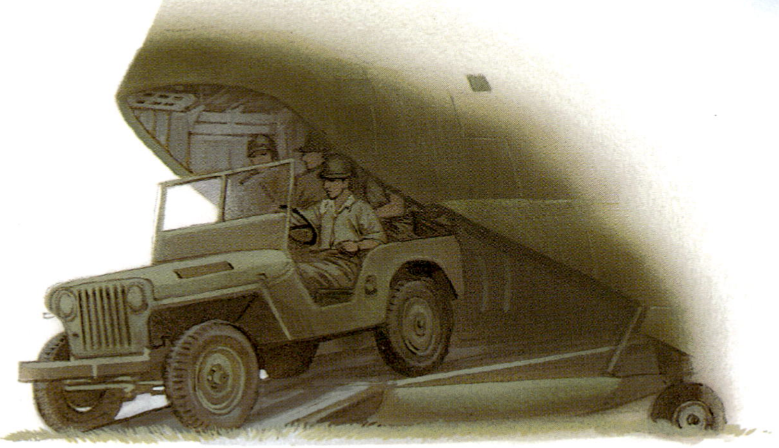

LOADING RAMP

With the rear loading ramp lowered, vehicles can be driven straight into and out of the helicopter. The Chinook can move small vehicles quickly by air to wherever they are needed.

ROTOR BLADES

The Chinook's twin-rotor layout, with rotor blades at each end, enables it to fly with a longer, more spacious fuselage than other helicopters. It is more stable, so it can lift heavy equipment on hooks underneath the fuselage. The long blades overlap, but they are arranged so that they cannot hit each other. They rotate in opposite directions so that the spinning forces that they apply to the helicopter cancel each other out. The rotor blades are made from fiberglass. Extra-tough titanium is used on the leading edges of the blades.

Stick boost actuators Provide extra power to operate the flying controls

Transmission shaft Transfers engine power to the front rotor

Fuel tank Holds 458gal. (2,068l) of fuel

Engine-intake screen Keeps dust and larger objects out of the engine

Drive shaft Links the engine to the rear rotor

The Chinook is unusual because it has two overhead rotors, one at the front and the other at the rear. Fuel is stored in the bulge running down each side of the fuselage. The helicopter weighs 22,379lb. (10,151kg) unladen.

Front rotor

Air data probes

Emergency exit window

TROOP SEATING

The Chinook is designed to carry 44 seated troops on a normal flight, although on one occasion, it carried 81 paratroopers! The bench-type seats are arranged down each side of the aircraft to save space, and are made from nylon sheet stretched over a tubular aluminum frame.

SKI SHOES

As a military aircraft, the Chinook has to be able to operate in all weather conditions. Its landing gear can be fitted with ski shoes for coming down on snow or ice. The broad surface of the ski shoes spreads the weight of the aircraft to stop it sinking into the ground.

TROOP LITTERS

The Chinook can be adapted for many uses. One of the Chinook's most important roles is evacuating casualties during wartime. It can be fitted with up to 22 litters (stretchers) stacked four deep, down each side of the fuselage.

PASSENGER SEATING

A civilian version of the Chinook was used to transport passengers. For example, it would take oil workers to offshore oil rigs. The bare military interior and seating were replaced by more comfortable airline-style seats. The Chinook is no longer used for civilian purposes.

S pyplane

"The windscreen gets so hot that a pilot can't keep his hand on it for more than 20 seconds even with flame-retardant gloves."
Captain Thomas L. Peterson, Blackbird pilot

The Lockheed SR-71 entered service in the 1960s as a high-altitude, ultra-fast spyplane. It is the world's first stealth aircraft, and holds the world air-speed record of 2,193mph (3,529kph). It flies at an altitude of 85,300ft. (26,000m), higher than most other aircraft. But more than this, the SR-71 can avoid detection on enemy radar screens because of its black, radar-absorbent paint and its unique shape. Its color has earned the SR-71 the name "Blackbird."

The preparations for each flight begin with two hours of preflight checks. While the aircrew, the pilot and a reconnaissance (spying) systems operator (RSO), put on their pressure suits, the ground crew starts up all the aircraft's systems – from electricity generators and computers to life-support systems. The crew climbs into the cramped cockpit nearly an hour before takeoff. At its maximum speed, its cameras photograph 100,000sq. mi. (259,000sq. km) of the ground every hour.

PRESSURE SUIT

Blackbirds fly at such great altitude that their pilots wear pressure suits and helmets similar to an astronaut's spacesuit. The suit completely seals the pilot inside. The suit has to be supplied with oxygen for the pilot to breathe.

Angled tail fin

Corrugated wing panel

Ejector flap to control exhaust airflow

SPY PHOTOS

Despite the speed at which it flies, clear photographs can be taken from Blackbird on its spy missions by panoramic and long-range cameras held in the main sensor bay. The picture above was taken on a practice flight and shows the Los Angeles coastline in California.

Main sensor bay

PARACHUTE

The Blackbird needs some help to stop from its touchdown speed of 173mph (278kph). A compartment in the top of the fuselage opens and a huge parachute streams out. The drag this creates slows the Blackbird to a halt within about 3,280ft. (1,000m).

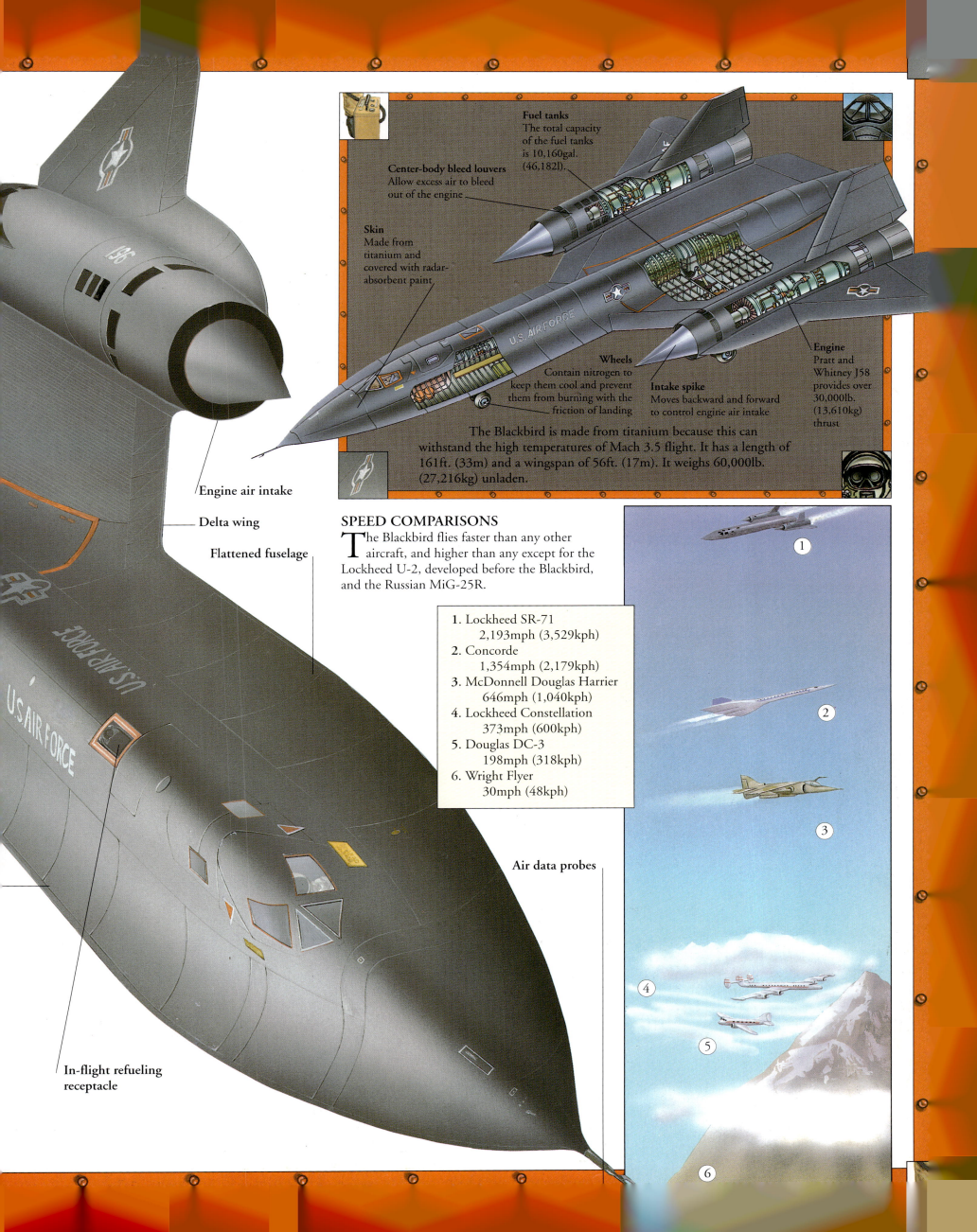

Fuel tanks
The total capacity
of the fuel tanks
is 10,160gal.
(46,182l).

Center-body bleed louvers
Allow excess air to bleed
out of the engine

Skin
Made from
titanium and
covered with radar-
absorbent paint

Wheels
Contain nitrogen to
keep them cool and prevent
them from burning with the
friction of landing

Intake spike
Moves backward and forward
to control engine air intake

Engine
Pratt and
Whitney J58
provides over
30,000lb.
(13,610kg)
thrust

U.S. AIR FORCE

The Blackbird is made from titanium because this can
withstand the high temperatures of Mach 3.5 flight. It has a length of
161ft. (33m) and a wingspan of 56ft. (17m). It weighs 60,000lb.
(27,216kg) unladen.

Engine air intake

Delta wing

Flattened fuselage

SPEED COMPARISONS

The Blackbird flies faster than any other
aircraft, and higher than any except for the
Lockheed U-2, developed before the Blackbird,
and the Russian MiG-25R.

1. Lockheed SR-71
2,193mph (3,529kph)
2. Concorde
1,354mph (2,179kph)
3. McDonnell Douglas Harrier
646mph (1,040kph)
4. Lockheed Constellation
373mph (600kph)
5. Douglas DC-3
198mph (318kph)
6. Wright Flyer
30mph (48kph)

U.S. AIR FORCE

Air data probes

In-flight refueling
receptacle

1
2
3
4
5
6

Hoverfly

"What's surprising . . . for an aircraft with such extraordinary flying characteristics . . . is it's very easy to fly."
Captain Charles "Chuck" Maloney,
American Harrier pilot

This unusual military aircraft was developed during the 1960s and first flew in 1967. The Harrier is capable of flying in ways that are impossible for other aircraft. It can take off and land vertically like a helicopter, which has earned it the name "Jump Jet." This means that it can be used during warfare even if runways are destroyed. It can also hover motionless in the sky and even fly backward! A single lever controls the position of the plane's engine nozzles, which gives this aircraft its special mobility. The nozzles are rotated to point downward or backward by moving the lever. Sitting on an ejector seat, the pilot commands this fast-attack aircraft from a cockpit with good all-around visibility. The Harrier can carry a selection of missiles and bombs. Two gun pods under the fuselage can each hold 100 shells.

FLYING GEAR

Harrier pilots wear a pressure suit with a life preserver, which inflates if they ditch in the sea. The suit also squeezes the pilot's legs when the Harrier makes sharp turns. This stops blood from draining from the pilot's head.

VERTICAL TAKEOFF

The arrows on the diagram above show the direction the plane is flying. Before the plane takes off, the engine nozzles point downward. The pilot opens the throttle near his left thigh to increase the engine's thrust, and the plane rises vertically. The pilot then rotates the engine nozzles until they point backward, and the blast of exhaust gases pushes the plane forward.

Cooling air intake

Rocket pod

Tail radar

05

MN

159246

MARINES

VMA231

Air brake

SKI JUMP

The Harrier can carry more fuel and weapons if it takes off from a runway instead of vertically. This is because vertical takeoff uses more power. The Harrier's takeoff run can be shortened by sloping the end of the runway upward. This is especially useful when Harriers operate from aircraft carriers. These ships have a sloped deck called a "ski jump." A Harrier with a heavy load can take to the air from this runway. On its return, and with a lighter load, the Harrier can land vertically. This is the safest way to land on a ship's deck.

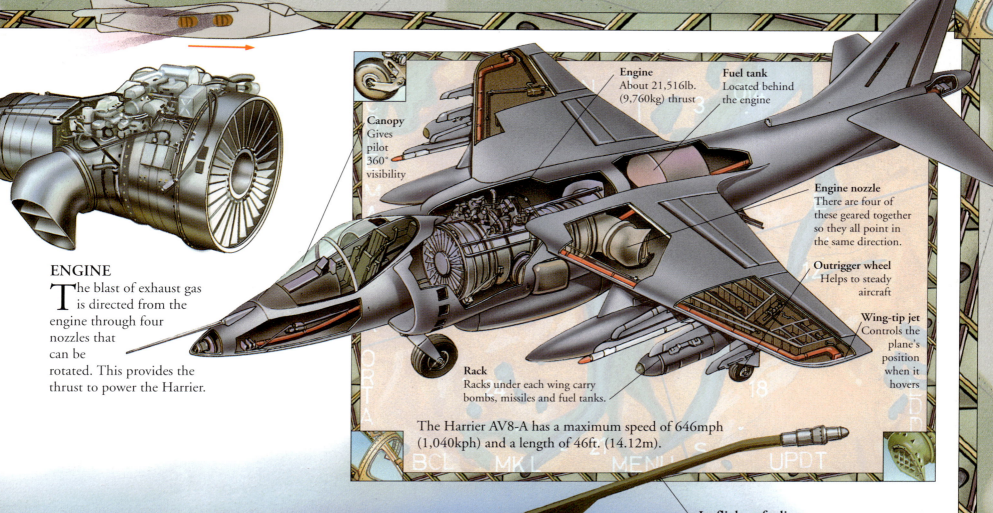

ENGINE

The blast of exhaust gas is directed from the engine through four nozzles that can be rotated. This provides the thrust to power the Harrier.

Canopy Gives pilot 360° visibility

Engine About 21,516lb. (9,760kg) thrust

Fuel tank Located behind the engine

Engine nozzle There are four of these geared together so they all point in the same direction.

Outrigger wheel Helps to steady aircraft

Wing-tip jet Controls the plane's position when it hovers

Rack Racks under each wing carry bombs, missiles and fuel tanks.

The Harrier AV8-A has a maximum speed of 646mph (1,040kph) and a length of 46ft. (14.12m).

Auxiliary air intake

In-flight refueling probe

Yaw vane

605

Cockpit air intake

Gun pod

CONTROL LEVERS

The nozzle lever controls the angle of the engine exhaust nozzles. The throttle increases the engine's thrust. The Short Takeoff Stop and Vertical Takeoff Stop mark the places for the nozzle lever to be positioned to take off from ski jumps (short takeoff), or to take off vertically.

1. Throttle
2. Short Takeoff Stop
3. Nozzle lever
4. Vertical Takeoff Stop

INSTRUMENT PANEL

Screens display radar warning, navigation and engine data, as well as the weapons status and a map that shows the land beneath the Harrier as it is flying. The most important data, such as speed, altitude and any possible threat, is projected on a glass plate, or "head-up display," in the pilot's line of sight.

111

Faster than sound

"It's the closest thing to space travel I'm ever likely to experience, yet it seemed so normal. Concorde really is a remarkable aircraft. It gives you the opportunity to be a shirt-sleeve astronaut."
Peter Johnson, a Concorde passenger

Concorde is the world's first supersonic commercial passenger aircraft operating regular scheduled flights. Concorde was developed jointly by Britain and France during the 1960s and 1970s, when the DC-3, the Constellation and the Comet 4s were in regular service. No other aircraft can match Concorde's dreamlike performance and comfort. Nor can any other aircraft fly faster than sound over great distances without requiring in-flight refueling. A few military aircraft can fly faster, but they need in-flight refueling to fly as far. Concorde flies high through the atmosphere on the edge of space. At an altitude of 12mi. (18km), flying at 1,354mph (2,179kph), passengers can see the curve of the earth's surface. But there is no sensation of speed. The aircraft seems to hang motionless in the air, yet the lightning speed makes the windows feel warm because of friction with the air outside.

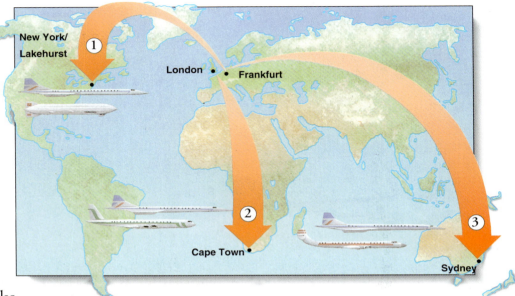

PASSENGER SERVICE

The above map shows how Concorde has improved flight times across the world. This ability to fly so quickly and in such style has made Concorde an important service for the business community.

1. Transatlantic route: 2 hr. 54.5 min. by Concorde, 65 hr. by *Hindenburg* airship
2. South African route: 8 hr. 8 min. by Concorde, 24 hr. by de Havilland Comet
3. Australian route: 17 hr. 13min. by Concorde, 55 hr. 7 min. by Lockheed Constellation

DROOP-SNOOT

Concorde's nose was designed to "droop," to give a clear view ahead for takeoff and landing (1). The nose is raised for normal flight (2).

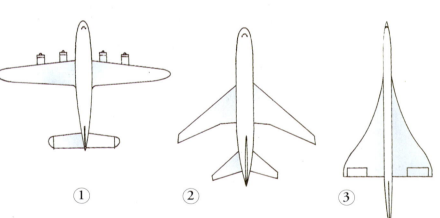

WING POSITIONS

The faster a plane is designed to fly, the more its wings have to be swept back. A piston-engined plane has straight wings (1). A jet airliner's wings are angled at 25-40 degrees (2). Concorde's wings are swept back so much that they form a triangular "delta" shape (3).

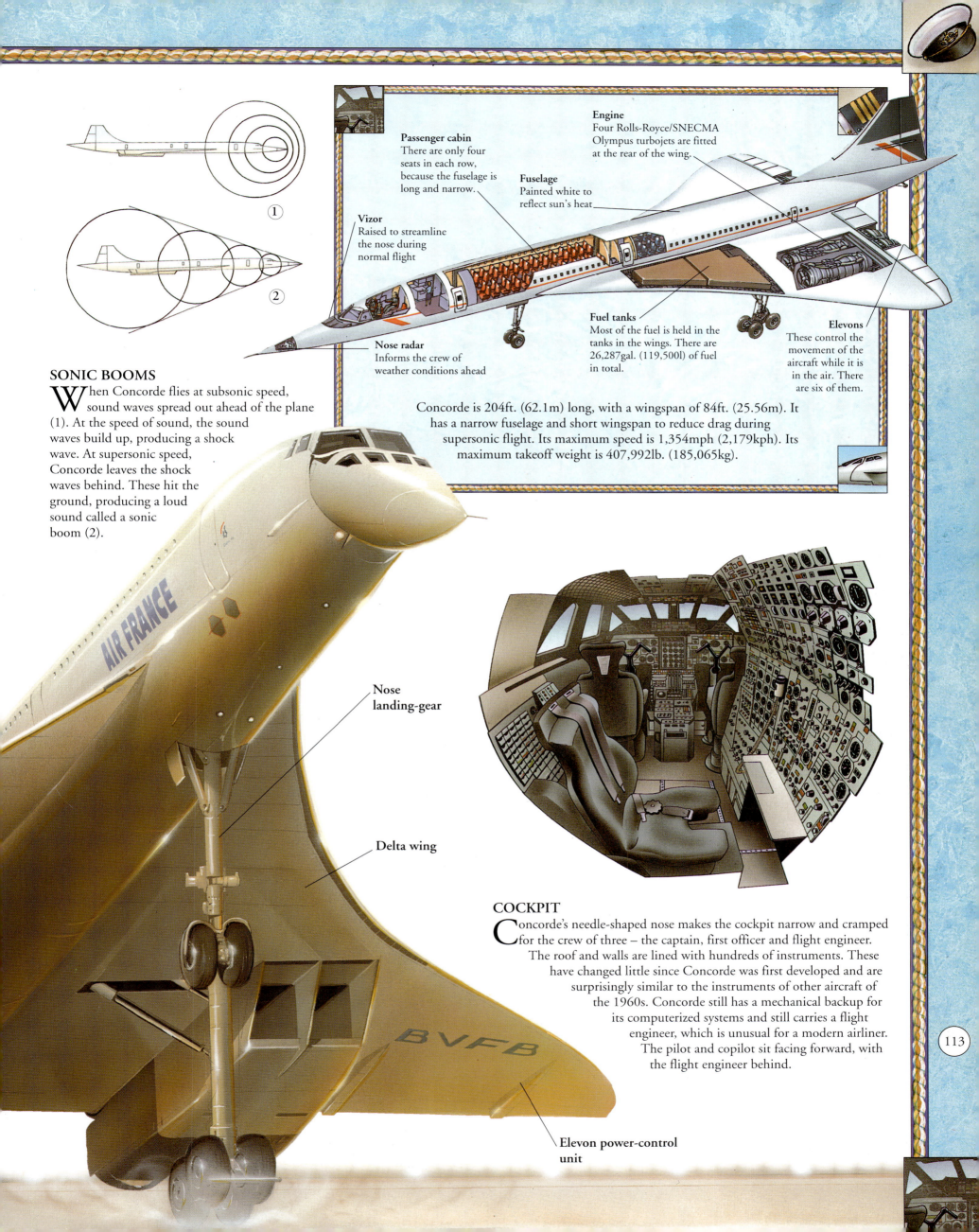

Engine
Four Rolls-Royce/SNECMA Olympus turbojets are fitted at the rear of the wing.

Passenger cabin
There are only four seats in each row, because the fuselage is long and narrow.

Fuselage
Painted white to reflect sun's heat

Vizor
Raised to streamline the nose during normal flight

Nose radar
Informs the crew of weather conditions ahead

Fuel tanks
Most of the fuel is held in the tanks in the wings. There are 26,287gal. (119,500l) of fuel in total.

Elevons
These control the movement of the aircraft while it is in the air. There are six of them.

Concorde is 204ft. (62.1m) long, with a wingspan of 84ft. (25.56m). It has a narrow fuselage and short wingspan to reduce drag during supersonic flight. Its maximum speed is 1,354mph (2,179kph). Its maximum takeoff weight is 407,992lb. (185,065kg).

SONIC BOOMS

When Concorde flies at subsonic speed, sound waves spread out ahead of the plane (1). At the speed of sound, the sound waves build up, producing a shock wave. At supersonic speed, Concorde leaves the shock waves behind. These hit the ground, producing a loud sound called a sonic boom (2).

Nose landing-gear

Delta wing

COCKPIT

Concorde's needle-shaped nose makes the cockpit narrow and cramped for the crew of three – the captain, first officer and flight engineer. The roof and walls are lined with hundreds of instruments. These have changed little since Concorde was first developed and are surprisingly similar to the instruments of other aircraft of the 1960s. Concorde still has a mechanical backup for its computerized systems and still carries a flight engineer, which is unusual for a modern airliner. The pilot and copilot sit facing forward, with the flight engineer behind.

Elevon power-control unit

The nighthawk

The Lockheed F-117A was designed to avoid detection by radar and also to mount precision attacks on its target. It is the world's first stealth combat aircraft. It is so difficult to detect either visually or by radar that it has earned the name "Nighthawk." The F-117A first flew in 1981 and first entered combat in 1989. It was designed not only to avoid detection by radar but also to mount precision attacks on its targets. The aircraft's pyramid shape is made up of many angled surfaces to reflect radar signals away from their source. It is made from a metal that is coated with a special material that also absorbs some of the radar signals that strike it. Once in the air, Nighthawk's computers fly it to within sight of the target so that the pilot can concentrate on delivering the weapons, which include air-to-air missiles and laser-guided bombs. Stealth fighters attack the most important and most heavily defended targets.

"We simply could not have done what we've done as effectively and efficiently, and at as low a cost to life, both our's and the enemy's, if we hadn't that stealth capability."
U.S. Secretary of Defense,
Dick Cheney, 1991

Butterfly tail fins

Flattened engine exhaust nozzle

Swept-back wing

SECURITY PALM PRINTS

Stealth fighters are protected by 24-hour security. Armed guards surround their hangars. An electronic security system checks authorized personnels' palm prints before they are allowed near the aircraft.

PAYLOAD

Stealth fighters are loaded with up to 5,000lb. (2,268kg) of weapons. The choice of weaponry available includes laser-guided bombs, air-to-air missiles and air-to-surface missiles. Two bombs or missiles are carried side by side on racks in the central weapons bay. Two different types of weapons can be carried at the same time.

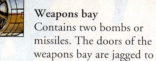

Weapons bay
Contains two bombs or missiles. The doors of the weapons bay are jagged to help deflect radar.

Engine
Two turbofan engines are deep inside the plane so their heat and vibration cannot be detected by missiles.

Canopy
With windshield made from radar-absorbing glass.

Engine air intake
Covered by rectangular grids. They shield the engines from radar waves.

The F-117A has a length of 65.6ft. (20m) and a wingspan of 43.3ft. (13.2m). Its maximum takeoff weight is 52,500lb. (23,814kg). It has a top speed of 593mph (955kph).

Radar-absorbent material

Pyramid-shaped cockpit

COCKPIT

The aircraft's pyramid shape leaves little headroom, but gives plenty of comfortable footroom for the pilot. The instrument panel was designed, where possible, to include components already manufactured for other military aircraft. Ready-made parts are easy to obtain and cheaper than custom-made components.

INVISIBLE SHAPE

The Nighthawk's curious shape, built up from carefully angled flat panels, enables it to avoid detection by enemy radar.

Forward Looking Infra Red (FLIR) system

Air data probes

115

Firebird

"No other aircraft can match it. It can race to a fire, scoop water from a nearby lake and "bomb" the fire with it up to 50 times over."

Louis Brennan,
firefighter and pilot

During the 1950s and 1960s small aircraft were adapted or designed for use in situations that were too dangerous or difficult for land vehicles. The CL-415, or "Firebird," is a modern example of this. It was developed by Canadair especially to fight raging forest fires that were impossible to reach by firefighters on the ground. Traveling up to a speed of 233mph (375kph), the CL-415 can get to the scene in a fraction of the time that would be taken by a land vehicle and with much less risk. It puts out fires by dropping water or foam on them from its built-in tanks. The CL-415 is amphibious – it can take off and land from both water and the ground. This means that it can use water sources such as lakes and the sea for firefighting. The CL-415 is very versatile. For example, it can be adapted to rescue people at sea or to spray chemicals on crops.

Engine air intake

Wing flap

SPRAY BOOM

A spray boom (a pipe with holes along its length) is fitted under each wing and attached to built-in tanks loaded with chemicals. This allows the CL-415 to be used for spraying pesticides on crops, or for spraying detergents to dissolve oilslicks.

SPRAYING CHEMICALS

The CL-415 flies across the direction of the wind, using the wind itself to spread the chemicals. A single aircraft can spray an area of 4,450 ha. (4,000 soccer fields) in just one flight.

WATER TANKS

The CL-415 can scoop 1,348gal. (6,130l) of water into its tanks in 12 seconds. Foam is added to the water because it smothers the fire quickly and is therefore more effective than water alone. To drop the water and foam on the fire, doors in the bottom of the tanks are opened using a control in the cockpit.

Turboprop engine
Pratt and Whitney PW123 engine mounted over wing clear of water

Water tanks
Hold 1,348gal. (6,130l) of water

Foldaway seats
These are used by the fire crew.

Main wheel
Retracts into fuselage

Storage tanks
These store the concentrated foam that is added to the water.

The CL-415 has a fuselage which is shaped like a boat's hull so that it can float. It is 65.6ft. (20m) long, with a wingspan of 95ft. (29m). Its maximum speed is 233mph (375kph).

Keel

Landing lights

SEA RESCUE

The CL-415 can search for survivors for up to seven hours without refueling. Unlike other aircraft used for rescue work, the CL-415 can land on the sea, and so people are taken straight on board instead of being hoisted into the air. There is room inside the CL-415 for three cabin crew and six survivors.

Float

AMPHIPORT

Amphibious aircraft, such as the CL-415, land on lakesides or marinas and taxi up a ramp on to firm ground to collect passengers. These collecting stations are known as amphiports.

Wing fence

GLOSSARY

aerial photograph
A photograph taken of the ground or of objects in the air, by a camera carried on aircraft.

aft
Used to describe the rear section of a ship.

aileron
A movable, hinged panel along the rear edge of each airplane wing. Ailerons swivel up or down. They always swivel in opposite directions. If one is up, the other is always down. Operating the ailerons makes the airplane roll to one side or the other.

aircraft carrier
A heavy warship designed to operate aircraft at sea from its flight deck.

airflow
The movement of air over and under a surface, such as a wing.

airfoil
The special curved shape of an airplane wing or helicopter rotor blade. The airfoil shape generates an upward force called lift.

airliner
A large airplane designed specifically to carry passengers.

air pressure
The pushing force exerted on an object caused by the weight of all the air above it. Air pressure is greatest on the ground, at the lowest part of the atmosphere. Air thins out and its pressure drops with increasing height.

airship
An aircraft that rises into the air because it is lighter than air. An airship is constructed from a metal frame containing bags filled with hydrogen or helium gas. The pilot flies the craft from a gondola attached to the bottom of the airship.

altitude
An aircraft's altitude is its height above sea level.

amidships
Steering the ship straight ahead.

amphibious aircraft
An aircraft that can take off from, and land on, either water or land. (Flying boats are not amphibious because they can operate from water but not from land.)

anchor
A weight or large hook dropped on a cable to the seabed to stop a ship from drifting.

a-port
Steering the ship to the left.

armored train
A train covered in protective metal and carrying guns for use in wartime.

artemon
An angled foremast carrying a spritsail. Used

before the adoption of the bowsprit in the sixteenth century.

articulated coach
A coach adjacent to another with a shared bogie.

articulated locomotive
A steam locomotive with two sets of cylinders, each driving a separate set of wheels, and each set pivoting on its own frame.

a-starboard
Steering the ship to the right.

ASW
"Anti-Submarine Warfare" or "Anti-Submarine Weapon": a depth charge, missile or hunting torpedo, used by surface ships against submarines.

asynchronous
An alternating-current (AC) electric motor whose speed varies with the load, not with the current supplied to it.

atmosphere
All the gases that surround the earth.

automatic mail collection and delivery
A system for collecting and delivering mail from a moving train.

B-B wheel notation
A description of a diesel or electric locomotive with two twin-axle driving bogies, each pair of axles being driven by one traction motor.

baker valve gear
A system of valve gears invented by Abner D. Baker in 1903 and modified in 1912 to replace the older Walschaert's valve gear. It used rods and bell cranks instead of link and sliding link blocks, making the gear more efficient and easier to service. Baker valve gear was found mostly on American steam trains built after 1912.

ballast tanks
Tanks which can be flooded and emptied to make a submarine dive and surface.

battle-cruiser
A battleship with reduced armor to enable it to travel at greater speed.

battleship
A heavily armored capital ship armed with guns which have bores greater than 8.5in. (22cm) in diameter.

beakhead
The pointed, enclosed space immediately in front of a sailing ship's forecastle.

beam
A ship's width from side to side.

belaying pin
Heavy wooden pin used to secure the ropes.

bilge
Long, narrow plates on the lowest part of a ship inside the hull.

biplane
An aircraft with two pairs of wings, one pair above the other. Biplanes were popular until the 1930s.

blast pipe
A vertical pipe fitted beneath the chimney inside the smokebox of a steam locomotive. It carries the exhaust steam from the cylinders and waste material from the fire into the atmosphere. This produces a partial vacuum in the smokebox, which improves the draft for the fire.

Bo-Bo-Bo wheel notation
A description of a diesel or electric locomotive with three twin-axle bogies, with each axle being individually driven.

bogie
A truck – a frame with wheels – that attaches to the underframe of a wagon, carriage or locomotive and allows it to turn on curved track.

boiler
The part of a steam locomotive, containing a firebox surrounded by water, that produces steam.

boiler pressure
The force exerted by the production of steam in the boiler of a steam locomotive.

bomber
An aircraft designed to carry bombs.

bomb rack
A frame that holds bombs inside a bomber aircraft's bomb bay.

boom
A spar used to keep a sail stretched, support extra sails or carry anti-torpedo netting.

boum
A two-masted Arab sailing ship with lateen sails.

bow
The front end of a ship. It is pointed in shape.

bow-post
The timber or metal frame rising from the front end of the keel.

bowsprit
A large spar extended from a ship's bow to support stays for the foremast, and a boom from which jibs or a spritsail can be rigged.

bracing wire
Tight wire stretched between a biplane's upper and lower wings and between the wings and the fuselage to hold the wings in place.

bridge
A platform above the upper deck, from which a ship is controlled.

broad gauge
Railroad track that is wider than the standard gauge, once used on express lines to allow trains to travel at greater speeds.

broadside
All the guns on one side of a ship, arranged to fire together.

bulkhead
A vertical wall dividing a ship's interior into separate compartments.

cab
The driver's compartment on a locomotive.

caboose
The last car at the end of a goods train, often called the guard's van. It has an observation platform at the back.

canopy
The clear, curved cover over an aircraft's cockpit. The canopy is usually made from a tough plastic.

capital ship
The heaviest type of powered warship, usually describing a battleship, battle-cruiser or aircraft carrier.

capstan
A winch consisting of a cylindrical drum around which cables are wound. Used for heavy lifting work.

caravel
A small sailing ship of the fifteenth and early sixteenth centuries, capable of being rigged with either lateen or square sails.

carriage
A railroad car that carries passengers.

carrying wheel
A wheel at the front or back of a bogie, before or after the driving wheels, which supports the engine but is not linked to the power supply by a connecting rod.

carvel
A shipbuilding technique in which the planks of the outer hull are laid edge to edge.

castle
A structure built up from the bow and stern of a medieval sailing ship, from which soldiers could defend the ship and attack other ships.

catamaran
A multi-hull sailing craft or ship, consisting of two hulls joined by a central platform.

ceiling
An aircraft's ceiling is the maximum height at which it can fly safely.

clinker
A shipbuilding technique in which the planks of the outer hull are laid with overlapping edges.

clipper
A high-speed sailing ship with a sharp, curved bow, designed to "clip" days off the journey time of other ships.

coach
Another name for carriage.

cockpit
The compartment at the front of an aircraft where the pilot and copilot sit. All of the flight controls are located in the cockpit.

collector shoe
A metal block on the underside of an electric train that slides along the top of an electrified third rail to collect current.

compound locomotive
A system for driving steam locomotives using both high pressure and low pressure cylinders. It was pioneered in France by Alfred De Glehn in the late nineteenth century.

connecting rod
A metal bar that connects the piston rod to the driving wheels of a steam locomotive.

conning tower
The structure above the outer casing from which a submarine is commanded when on the surface of the water.

console
The panel in front of the pilot containing the instruments used when flying.

corridor connection
A short flexible corridor connected between railroad carriages that enables passengers to walk the length of a train.

corridor tender
A corridor fitted to the inside of a steam locomotive tender that enables the crew to pass between the cab and the rest of the train. It was once used by some rail companies on their long-distance nonstop express trains to allow a fresh crew to take over during the journey.

counterstern
A ship's stern which is high and curved, instead of square.

course
The largest, lowest sail supported by a ship's mast.

cowcatcher
A V-shaped metal frame at the front of a locomotive that pushes obstacles off the track.

cowling
A removable outer cover which is used to protect an engine.

cradle
Part of an early Wright brothers' airplane. This is where the pilot lay, and from where he steered the aircraft.

cruise missile
A very accurate flying bomb. After it is fired from a ship or dropped from an aircraft, a cruise missile flies under the power of its own jet engine. It steers itself toward the target with pinpoint accuracy by comparing its view of the ground via a built-in television camera with a map stored in its computer memory.

cruising speed
The speed at which an aircraft normally flies.

cylinder
One of the chambers inside a piston engine where fuel and air are compressed and burned to provide power.

de-icing
The removal of ice from an aircraft while it is flying. In some weather conditions, ice can form on an aircraft's windows and wings. Ice building up on a wing's smooth curved shape can affect its ability to create the lifting force that keeps the plane in the air. An airliner's flight-deck windows are electrically heated and the leading edges of the wings are heated by air from the engines to prevent ice from forming.

deck beam
The beams running from side to side in a ship, supporting the decks.

destroyer
A fast, light warship, originally intended to "destroy" enemy torpedo boats, with a combined surface, anti-submarine and anti-aircraft role.

dhow
Name for a lateen-rigged Arab sailing ship.

diesel electric
A locomotive powered by the electric current produced by a generator driven by a diesel engine.

director
Control center for directing the fire of a warship's guns.

displacement
The weight of a ship, measured by the tons of water displaced when the ship is afloat.

dogfight
A battle in the air at close quarters, between fighter planes. The planes twist and turn in the air at great speed in an attempt to train their guns on each other. The Sopwith Camels were particularly good at dogfighting.

dome car
A passenger coach fitted with a protruding glass roof that gives passengers views of the scenery.

drag
A force caused by air resistance that acts to slow an aircraft down.

draught
The depth of water between the bottom of a ship's hull and the waterline when afloat, varying with the weight of its load.

dreadnought
A battleship designed to carry eight or more heavy guns, named after HMS *Dreadnought*, first of the type (1906).

driving wheel
One of the wheels of a locomotive that is connected to the power supply and makes the locomotive move forward.

dynamometer car
A carriage fitted with equipment for measuring and recording the horsepower and speed of a locomotive at work.

electrical induction
The production of an electric current by a change of magnetic field.

electro-pneumatic brakes
Air-pressure brakes that are activated by electricity.

elevator
A movable hinged panel along each rear edge of an aircraft's tail plane. When both strips swivel up, the plane tilts tail-down. When they swivel down, the tail is pushed up. Elevators make a plane soar or dive.

fighter
A small, fast and well-armed aircraft designed to find and attack other aircraft.

figurehead
A painted statue mounted on a ship's bow, usually referring to the ship's name.

firebox
The part of a steam locomotive where coal or logs are burned.

flanged wheel
A wheel fitted with a projecting inside rim that makes a train stay on the track.

flap
A movable section at the back of a wing, extended backward to generate more lift on takeoff and before landing.

flight deck
The part at the front of an aircraft where the pilot and other crew sit. A flight deck is larger than a cockpit.

flight engineer
Aircraft used to be flown by a crew of three – the pilot, the copilot and the flight engineer. The flight engineer monitored the engines during a flight. Nowadays, computers normally monitor engines, so flight engineers are not needed. Concorde, however, still has a flight engineer.

footplate
The floor in the driver's cab of a steam locomotive where the driver and fireman stood.

fore
The word used to describe the front, or forward, section of a ship.

forecastle (or fo'c's'le)
The space in the bow beneath a ship's short raised forward deck: traditionally the living quarters of the crew.

foremast
The mast of a sailing ship nearest to the bow.

frigate
A fast, light warship used to scout for the main battle fleet; nowadays mainly designed for ASW.

funnel
A large ventilator tube for carrying away the heat, smoke and fumes from a ship's furnaces and engines. Also called a smokestack.

fuselage
The body of an aircraft, running from nose to tail. The fuselage contains the cockpit or flight deck, the cargo hold and the passenger cabin.

galley
A ship's kitchen or a food preparation area in an aircraft. Also a light, narrow warship driven by oars.

gauge
The distance between the inner faces of the rails of railroad track. This is usually 4 feet 8.5 inches (143.5 centimeters), but nonstandard gauges may be narrower or wider than this.

glider
An aircraft without an engine. Gliders are towed into the air by a powered aircraft or by a tow-line attached to a winch on the ground, and soar higher on rising currents of air.

gondola
The crew compartment that hangs underneath an airship.

gradient
A measurement of a slope or hill, usually expressed as a percentage or a ratio. A gradient of 1 in 50 (up), or 2 percent, means that the slope rises 1 unit in height (either feet or meters) for every 50 units of distance. The closer the ratio or the higher the percentage, the steeper the gradient; 1 in 50 is steep for a main line.

grate
The part of a steam locomotive firebox that contains the fuel for the fire.

gun port
Square hole cut in a ship's side for a gun to fire through.

headwind
A wind blowing on to the bow of a ship, making progress difficult.

high pressure
The pressure of steam in a boiler of a steam locomotive (always measured in pounds) when it exceeds 200lb per square inch.

horsepower
A unit of power equal to 33,000 feet per pound per minute (75 kilograms per meter per second), or 746 watts.

hub
The central part of a wheel or propeller.

hull
The main, watertight body of a boat, ship, submarine, or flying boat. Consisting of the upper deck, the sides and the bottom.

hydraulic
Powered by the pressure of oil forced through pipes by a pump.

hydrofoil
A ship that can be lifted clear of the water by an angled plane, or foil, when travelling at high speed.

island
The superstructure of an aircraft carrier, with bridge, funnels and masts, usually placed on the starboard side of the flight deck.

jet engine
An engine that uses a jet of gas to push an aircraft through the air. The jet is produced by sucking air into the front of the engine, compressing it and mixing it with burning fuel. This causes the air to expand rapidly, and it rushes out of the back of the engine as a powerful exhaust.

jib
A small triangular sail set between the foremast and the bowsprit.

junk
A Chinese sailing ship with three or more masts and matting sails stiffened with bamboo slats.

keel
A ship's backbone: the lowest and strongest timber or line of metal plates of the hull, stretching the full length of the ship's underside.

knot
A measurement of a ship's speed. A knot is the equivalent to one nautical mile, or 1.15mph (1.853kph).

lateen sail
A large triangular sail, rigged fore and aft instead of from side to side.

leading edge
The front of a wing, tail fin or tail plane.

lift
The upward force on a wing, created by the airflow passing over it.

liner
A large, fast passenger ship belonging to the fleet of a shipping line.

locomotive
The engine unit of a train, which can be disconnected from the rest of the train.

loop
A railroad track that gains height by turning in a full circle and crossing over itself at a higher level.

mach number
To measure the speed of a supersonic aircraft Mach numbers are used. This is because the speed of sound is not the same everywhere in the atmosphere. Mach 1 is the speed of sound.

maglev
Magnetic levitation – a way of powering a train using magnetic attraction or repulsion instead of wheels attached to a power supply.

mainmast
The tallest and strongest central mast of a sailing ship, between the foremast and the mizzenmast.

marshaling yard
An area where railroad goods wagons are sorted and linked up to form complete trains.

mast
A tall, vertical spar for carrying sails and, nowadays, radio and radar aerials.

mechanical stoker
A device used in large steam locomotives that conveyed coal from the tender to the firebox.

mizzenmast
A sailing ship's rearmost mast, astern of the mainmast.

multi-hull
A ship designed for stability and speed, with more than one hull (two in a catamaran, three in a trimaran) joined above the water. Ferries are multi-hulled.

multiple unit
A train consisting of two or more powered units coupled together and operated by one driver.

multitube boiler
A steam boiler in which heat is taken through many tubes to heat the water more effectively.

narrow gauge
Railroad track that is narrower than standard gauge, often used in difficult terrain.

navigator
A crew member whose job was to plot an aircraft's course on long flights. After World War II, navigation aids using radio and radar enabled pilots to keep their craft on course, and so navigators were no longer needed.

navvy
A laborer who worked on canals and railroads.

observation car
The coach of a passenger train, usually at the rear, providing large windows for scenic viewing.

outrigger
A structure built outward from a ship's side.

outrigger wheel
A small wheel at or near the end of an aircraft's wing, used to steady the aircraft and stop its wing tips from touching the ground.

pannier tank
One of two or more tanks on a steam locomotive that carry the water supply in containers on both sides of the boiler.

pantograph
The spring-loaded and pivoted framework that links the top of an electric locomotive with its overhead power supply line.

periscope
A long tube with viewing glasses, for seeing above the water's surface from inside a submarine.

pigeon hole
One of a row of small compartments used for sorting letters in a traveling post-office train.

piston engine
An engine, similar to a car engine, that works by burning fuel inside cylinders. Hot gases push a piston down the cylinder to generate power to turn a propeller.

pitch
One of the three ways in which an aircraft can move. The other two are roll and yaw. Using the elevators in the tail to tilt the aircraft's nose up or down causes a change in pitch.

poopdeck
The shortest, uppermost deck of a ship, located at the stern.

power car
A car that contains an electric train's power supply. It is the equivalent of the engine, although it may propel the train from either end. Electric trains often have two power cars, one at each end.

preflight checks
Checks made before takeoff to ensure that the flaps are moving correctly, the engines are running smoothly and all the instruments are working properly.

pressure suit
Pilots of high-flying fighters, bombers and spyplanes wear a pressure suit. It inflates automatically like a balloon when the aircraft turns sharply, to stop blood from draining away from the pilot's head into the legs. Pilots who fly at the highest level wear a pressure suit that looks like an astronaut's spacesuit. The suit, a helmet and gloves completely cover the pilot.

pressurized
When something is raised to a higher pressure than normal it is pressurized. The cabins in airliners are pressurized. Airliners fly at heights where the air is too thin for passengers to breathe, so the air pressure in the cabin is raised in order that passengers can breathe normally.

propeller
A set of thin, angled blades attached to a central hub on an aircraft. When the hub spins, the angled blades force air backward, which pushes the aircraft forward. Also a rotating screw, usually with two, three or four blades, which drives a steamship through the water.

pullman car
A type of luxury car invented in 1859 by George Pullman in America. It was the world's first sleeper car.

quarterdeck
The upper deck of a ship, astern of the mainmast.

radar
A device used to detect the position of objects by measuring the echo of radio signals beamed at them. The letters of the word radar stand for RAdio Detection And Ranging.

radio telephone
A telephone system that works by using radio waves instead of fixed transmission wires.

radome
A dome-shaped cover made from a material through which radio waves can pass, used to protect radar equipment inside it.

ram
A pointed, strengthened extension of the keel at the bow, for smashing and sinking enemy ships.

regenerative brakes
A braking system used on DC electric locomotives in which the traction motors work as generators and put energy back into the supply system.

regulator
The valve on a steam locomotive that controls the amount of steam passing from the boiler to the cylinders, thus controlling the speed.

rheostatic braking
An electrical braking system used on the driving axles of modern high-speed trains. The traction motors act as generators, producing electrical energy that is absorbed by the wheels. This system does not need any outside power supply and so it can be used in emergencies.

rib
The parts of a wing's frame that run from the front of the wing to the back.

rigging
All ropes and cables used to support a ship's spars and to control the sails.

rivet
A metal peg used to hold two pieces of metal together. The process of fitting rivets is called riveting.

"ro-ro" ferry
A ferry designed for vehicles to "roll on" at one end of the ship and "roll off" at the other.

roll
One of the three ways in which an aircraft can move. The other two are pitch and yaw. Using the ailerons to raise one wing and lower the other makes an aircraft roll.

rolling stock
Any railroad car that is not an engine or a power car and cannot propel itself.

rotor
The rotating blades of a helicopter. Each rotor blade is like a long, thin wing. Most helicopters have two rotors, a larger main rotor on top to lift the craft into the air and a smaller rotor in the tail to stop the craft from spinning.

roundel
A circular identifying mark on an aircraft.

royal
A small sail, set above the topgallant.

121

rudder
A hinged flat timber or plate, hung from the sternpost of a ship and turned from side to side to change the ship's direction. Also a swiveling panel in an aircraft's vertical tail fin. Turning the rudder makes the tail swing around to the left or right.

running rigging
All moving ropes and cables used to control a ship's sails.

saddle tank
A type of tank on a steam locomotive. It carries the water supply in a large curved container around the top half of the boiler.

safety valve
A device fitted to the boiler of a steam locomotive that automatically releases excess steam when a certain pressure is reached.

SAM
A "Surface-to-Air Missile" for shooting down enemy aircraft.

sanding gear
A device fitted to locomotives that drops sand onto the rails to prevent the wheels slipping.

self-propelled
A vehicle, such as a railroad gun or crane, that contains its own power unit enabling it to move.

ship of the line
A sailing battleship with two or more gun-decks, powerful enough to join the line of battle.

shrouds
The ropes or sails rigged from the sides of the ship to support the masts.

sight
A device used by the crew to aim a gun or to aim bombs at a target on the ground.

signal
A warning device at the side of the track to control the safe movement of trains. A combination of mechanical arms and/or colored lights are used and controlled from a central signal box.

skids
A pair of long, thin runners fitted to the underside of a helicopter.

skysail
A small upper sail, set above the royal.

slat
A panel that extends from the front of the wing to make the wing bigger. This generates more lift so that the aircraft can land or take off more safely at low speeds.

sleeper (tie)
A beam made of timber, steel or concrete that holds the rails to the correct gauge and distributes the load of the train to the ballast below.

smokebox
The front section of a steam locomotive's boiler that contains the steam pipes to the cylinders, the blast pipe and the chimney.

sonar
From "SOund NAvigation and Ranging." A device used for locating submerged submarines with pulses of sound.

sonic boom
When an aircraft flies faster than the speed of sound, the air in front of the aircraft is compressed so much that it forms a shock wave that travels out through the air and even reaches the ground. As the shock wave passes by, people hear it as a double bang called a sonic boom.

sortie
A mission flown by a military aircraft.

spanker
A large four-sided sail. The lowest sail set from the mizzenmast.

spar
All pole supports used in a ship, including masts, yards and booms. Also part of the frame inside an aircraft wing that supports the wing's weight. Spars are strong tubes or beams that lie along the length of wings, from wing tip to wing tip.

spark arrester
A metal mesh that is fitted to the top of a steam locomotive's chimney to prevent the emission of hot coals and sparks.

spike
A heavy square section nail that holds the rail to the sleeper.

spoiler
A panel in the wing which can be raised to spoil the flow of air over the wing. Spoilers are used to slow an aircraft down and increase its rate of descent before landing.

spritsail
A four-sided sail set from an artemon or bowsprit.

square rig
An arrangement of four-sided sails, set from yards running across the ship from side to side.

SSM
A "Surface-to-Surface Missile," fired at enemy ships.

standing rigging
All fixed ropes and cables that support a ship's spars.

stealth aircraft
A stealth aircraft is one designed so that it is difficult to detect by radar. It is carefully shaped so that radio waves that hit it are not reflected back from where they came. It is also covered with a special coating that absorbs radio waves and weakens the reflections.

stern
The back end of a ship.

streamlining
A specially designed smooth shape applied to locomotives and coaches to reduce wind resistance when traveling at high speed. Streamlined trains became popular in the 1930s. Some of the same principles were applied to the modern aerodynamic designs of high-speed trains such as the Shinkansen, TGV and *Eurostar*.

stroke
A measurement of the distance that a piston travels when it moves up and down.

studdingsail
A small extra sail, supported from a boom extended from the outer end of a yard.

submarine
A ship armed with tubes for firing torpedoes or missiles. It is able to dive, operate below and return to the surface of the sea.

superelevated
A curved two-rail track with one rail raised above the level of the other rail, enabling trains to tilt and to move safely at high speeds.

supersonic
Faster than the speed of sound. The speed of sound changes when the air temperature changes. As the air is colder higher up in the atmosphere, the speed of sound changes also with height. At sea level, it is 761mph (1,225kph).

superstructure
The upper section of a powered ship, rising from the level of the top deck, including the bridge and funnel mountings.

switchback
A section of track that enables trains to zigzag up the side of a steep slope by alternately driving into a dead end and then backing out and up.

tail fin
The vertical part of an aircraft's tail. The rear part of the fin is hinged so that it can swivel, forming a rudder.

tanker
A cargo ship designed to carry liquid cargoes such as crude or refined oil, or liquid gas.

taxiing
An aircraft is taxiing when it is moving on the ground under its own power.

tender
A car connected to the engine of a steam locomotive that carries the fuel and water supply.

third rail
An extra rail alongside the two running rails that carries electric current to an electric train. It is an alternative to the pantograph.

thrust
The force produced by a jet engine that pushes an aircraft along.

tiller
The lever that turns the rudder from side to side.

titanium
A metal used to build the fastest aircraft. Air rubbing against the outer skin of an aircraft heats the metal up. Most aircraft are made from aluminum, which melts at 1,803°F (660°C). An aluminum plane flying at three times the speed of sound would melt. Planes that fly this fast are made from titanium, which melts at 3,669°F (1,660°C).

topgallant
A sail set above the topsail.

topsail
A sail set above the course.

torpedo
A missile fired to sink an enemy ship by exploding beneath the waterline.

torque
Twisting or turning caused by the rotation of blades, such as in a helicopter.

traction motor
A motor that makes wheels turn when they are supplied with electric power.

tractive effort
A measurement of the force exerted by a locomotive at its driving wheels. This is the standard way of measuring a locomotive's power, because performance varies so much with weather and track conditions, the size of the load, the gradient, and other factors.

traductor arm
A movable metal arm, used on traveling post-office trains, that suspended mail bags for delivery while the train was moving.

train
A series of vehicles on flanged wheels, pulled along a track by an engine or power car.

transformer
A device that changes the voltage of an electric current without changing its frequency.

traverse
A curved section of railroad track that enables a rail-mounted gun barrel to be moved horizontally.

trimaran
A multi-hull sailing craft or powered ship, of three hulls joined by a central platform above the water.

trireme
A Greek war galley rowed by three levels, or banks, of oars.

turbine
A wheel with angled blades. The turbine spins when a liquid or gas strikes the blades.

turboshaft engine
A type of jet engine used by helicopters. The jet of gas from the engine spins a turbine, which turns the rotor blades.

U-boat
German term for a submarine, from *Unterseeboot*, meaning "under sea boat."

ULCC
"Ultra-Large Crude Carrier": used for supertankers of more than 300,000 tons displacement.

undercarriage
An aircraft's wheels – also known as landing gear.

valve
A device that moves to create an opening to let steam, water or gas in or out.

variable pitch
The angle of an aircraft's propeller blades can be changed. This is known as variable pitch. Changing the angle of the blades increases or decreases the thrust produced by the propeller. One angle is best suited to slow flying speeds, another to fast cruising at high altitudes.

VLCC
"Very Large Crude Carrier": used for supertankers of 200,000–300,000 tons displacement.

wagon
A railroad car that carries freight.

walschaert's valve gear
A device that controls the distribution of steam in the steam chest of a locomotive cylinder. It was invented by a Belgian railroad engineer, Egide Walschaert, in 1844 and subsequently used by many railroads around the world.

water scoop
A mechanical device that was lowered from a steam locomotive tender to collect water from troughs while the train was moving fast.

water trough
A long metal channel, containing water and positioned centrally between the railroad track, that enabled steam locomotives to collect water while traveling at high speed.

westinghouse vacuum brake
An automatic braking system operated by atmospheric air pressure. The vacuum brake was invented by an American engineer, George Westinghouse, in 1871.

wheel arrangement
The way in which the driving wheels and carrying wheels are positioned on the bogies of a steam locomotive. Engineers kept changing the numbers and kinds of wheels on locomotives to try to achieve maximum performance, so there is no standard number or order of wheels. The most common way of describing wheel arrangement is the Whyte system, invented in 1900. In this system, the wheels are numbered in pairs from the front of the train, two on each side, so that 4-4-2 means 4 carrying wheels, 4 driving wheels, and 2 more carrying wheels. The carrying wheels may also be called leading and trailing wheels. 2-6-0 means 2 leading wheels, 6 driving wheels and no trailing wheels behind the driving wheels. Wheel arrangement is characteristic of particular classes of trains; for example, a popular arrangement in the 1930s was the 4-6-2 or "Pacific" arrangement. Diesel and electric locomotives have different notation systems. Bo-Bo is a diesel configuration of two sets of 4-wheel bogies with each axle being individually driven. The letters denote driving axles, so that A is 1, B is 2, C is 3; and axles individually driven are designated "0".

wheelbase
The distance between the outer driving wheels of a locomotive, measured from the point at which the wheels make contact with the rails. A locomotive with a short wheelbase (for example, a 0-4-0) is able to travel around sharper bends than a locomotive with a long wheelbase (such as a 4-8-4). Pivoting unpowered bogies, or trucks, are positioned at the front and rear of locomotives to help long engines to travel around curves.

wheelhouse
Large airships built in the 1930s were steered by turning large wheels. The cabin in which these wheels were located was called the wheelhouse.

wing fence
A vertical strip running from front to back on an aircraft wing. The wing fence is designed to improve the airflow over the wing so that it creates the maximum lift.

wing strut
A wooden or metal post that links the upper and lower wings of a biplane and holds them the correct distance apart.

wing-warping
The Wright brothers used wing-warping to steer the first aircraft. The pilot pulled wires to bend the wing tips and change the airflow over them.

yacht
A sail or powered vessel used for pleasure.

yard
A large spar hung from the mast, running across the ship from side to side, from which a sail is set.

yaw
One of the three ways in which an aircraft can move. The other two are pitch and roll. Turning the rudder causes the aircraft's nose to turn, or yaw, to the left or right.

INDEX